Great Careers

Sales, Marketing, Business, and Finance

with a High School Diploma

Titles in the *Great Careers* series

Great Careers

Sales, Marketing, Business, and Finance

with a High School Diploma

Paul Stinson

Ferguson Publishing

An imprint of Infobase Publishing

Great Careers with a High School Diploma
Sales, Marketing, Business, and Finance

Ferguson
An imprint of Infobase Publishing
132 West 31st Street
New York, NY 10001

ISBN-13:978-0-8160-7051-0

Library of Congress Cataloging-in-Publication Data

Great careers with a high school diploma. — 1st ed.
    v. cm.
  Includes bibliographical references and index
  Contents: [1] Food, agriculture, and natural resources — [2] Construction and trades — [3] Communications, the arts, and computers —
[4] Sales, marketing, business, and finance — [5] Personal care services, fitness, and education — [6] Health care, medicine, and science —
[7] Hospitality, human services, and tourism — [8] Public safety, law, and security — [9] Manufacturing and transportation — [10] Armed forces.
  ISBN-13: 978-0-8160-7046-6 (v.1)
  ISBN-10: 0-8160-7046-6 (v.1)
  ISBN-13: 978-0-8160-7043-5 (v.2)
  ISBN-10: 0-8160-7043-1 (v.2)
[etc.]
1. Vocational guidance — United States. 2. Occupations — United States.
3. High school graduates — Employment — United States.
  HF5382.5.U5G677 2007
  331.702'330973 — dc22

                                                              2007029883

You can find Ferguson on the World Wide Web at
http://www.fergpubco.com

Produced by Print Matters, Inc.
Text design by A Good Thing, Inc.
Cover design by Salvatore Luongo

Printed in the United States of America

Sheridan PMI 10 9 8 7 6 5 4 3 2

This book is printed on acid-free paper.

Contents

How to Use This Book

This book, part of the Great Careers with a High School Diploma series, highlights in-demand careers that require no more than a high school diploma or the general educational development (GED) credential and offer opportunities for personal growth and professional advancement to motivated readers who are looking for a field that's right for them. The focus throughout is on the fastest-growing jobs with the best potential for advancement in the field. Readers learn about future prospects while discovering jobs they may never have heard of.

Knowledge—of yourself and about a potential career—is a powerful tool in launching yourself professionally. This book tells you how to use it to your advantage, explore job opportunities, and identify a good fit for yourself in the working world.

Each chapter provides the essential information needed to find not just a job but a career that draws on your particular skills and interests. All chapters include the following features:

- ✴ "Is This Job for You?" presents a set of questions for you to answer about yourself to help you learn if you have what it takes to work in a given career.
- ✴ "Let's Talk Money" and "Lets Talk Trends" provide at a glance crucial information about salary ranges and employment prospects.
- ✴ "What You'll Do" provides descriptions of the essentials of each job.
- ✴ "Where You'll Work" relates the details of the settings and the rules and patterns typical of that field.
- ✴ "Your Typical Day" provides details about what a day on the job involves for each occupation.
- ✴ "The Inside Scoop" presents firsthand information from someone working in the field.
- ✴ "What You Can Do Now" provides advice on getting prepared for your future career.
- ✴ "What Training You'll Need" discusses state requirements, certifications, and courses or other training you may need as you get started on your new career path.
- ✴ "How to Talk Like a Pro" defines a few key terms that give a feel for the occupation.

- ✴ "How to Find a Job" gives the practical how-tos of landing a position.
- ✴ "Secrets for Success" and "Reality Check" share inside information on getting ahead.
- ✴ "Some Other Jobs to Think About" lists similar related careers to consider.
- ✴ "How You Can Move Up" outlines how people in each occupation turn a job into a career, advancing in responsibility and earnings power.
- ✴ "Web Sites to Surf" lists Web addresses of trade organizations and other resources providing more information about the career.

In addition to a handy comprehensive index, the back of the book features an appendix providing invaluable information on job hunting strategies and techniques. This section provides general tips on interviewing, constructing a strong résumé, and gathering professional references. Use this book to discover a career that seems right for you—the tools to get you where you want to be are at your fingertips.

Introduction

Young people who choose a career path in retail, sales, or finance often do so because they've got a nose for business or the hustle required for turning entrepreneurial spirit into a paycheck, or maybe even, someday, a business of their own. Whether it's a financial clerk making sure that all the employees get paid on time or a customer service agent addressing the concerns of a valued customer, workers in the fields of retail, sales, and finance take great satisfaction in being a part of a thriving career world that offers endless possibilities for growth and advancement.

As part of one of the largest vocational fields in the United States, the business careers covered in this volume account for more than 12.4 million jobs. Of those, about 4.3 million are held in retail sales careers, while another 4.1 million belong to the business support careers of secretary and administrative assistant, according to 2006 figures from the U.S. Bureau of Labor Statistics.

For high school graduates, the fields of retail, sales, and finance can be a great resource for self-education and the development of business skills. In many cases, you can learn the required skills on the job. For more complex jobs, such as a dispatcher, account collector, or certain financial positions, you may need to enroll in a specialized training program or achieve a certain level of certification in order to do your job. But unlike a degree program, the training for these positions can often be completed in just a few months, or even weeks. Plus, once you start working in specialized positions within these careers, many employers will pay for additional training, providing a deeper knowledge base in the pursuit of your goals.

More important, the job outlook for retail, sales, and finance careers looks promising in the coming years. According to Bureau of Labor Statistics projections, employment in service, management, business, and financial occupations will increase by a combined 7.5 million jobs between 2004 and 2014.

In fact, three of the 20 fastest-growing occupations will be in retail, service, and administrative support positions. Specifically, between 2004 and 2014, employment opportunities will increase by about:

- ✴ 17 percent for retail salespersons
- ✴ 26 percent for customer service representatives
- ✴ 26 percent for receptionists and information clerks

Credit the unquenchable thirst of businesses to expand operations and improve customer service for the projected growth. Increasingly, businesses are trying to separate themselves from their competitors by the quality of service they provide. That service could be on the sales floor as a retail associate, in the realm of customer care as a customer service representative, or as a shipping and receiving clerk. There are also the professions in the field of sales, retail, and finance that are a bit more behind-the-scenes, including financial clerk, account or bill collectors, secretaries, administrative assistants, and receptionists. Key to all of the careers we'll detail in this volume is the skill of managing information—mastery of this skill plays a crucial role in ensuring the smooth operation of businesses big and small.

Whether it's the retail field of production and shipping, the work of a customer service representative, or a job as a telemarketing professional, many professions that were once straightforward in their job description now rely heavily on those who have the know-how to handle basic computer programs and swiftly navigate the Internet and other information resources to help coworkers and customers alike.

As many businesses seek to expand their customer base, many are investing heavily in developing an online presence that requires considerable staff support from the fields of shipping and receiving, telemarketing, and customer service. Retail, however, isn't the only field that's seen its job description change with the times. The traditional secretary or administrative assistant who once took dictation or wrote letters for much of the day is now frequently asked to perform research tasks and act as a library of information on how to use the latest office technology.

Some professions allow for growth by the awarding of designations for completing courses or successfully taking exams. Secretaries, for example, can start on a path to becoming a certified administrative professional. For every step you take to learn while you're on the job, you become a more attractive candidate for getting promoted up the ladder. Although specialized courses are available in many of the fields we'll discuss in the book, there's no need to put your life on hold.

In many cases, all the training you'll need is often provided while you're on the job. This training could include learning a bank's operating system or code of conduct for bank tellers, or it could include going through a one-week telemarketing training program that helps employees learn various sales techniques. On the other hand, it could be just a brief store or product overview from a store manager before you hit the sales floor as a retail associate. While the job descriptions will vary, workers in retail, sales, and finance all share one common goal: managing information. Depending on the job title, your job is to keep track of the information that's vital to the functioning of your business. Whether it's people or products, a large part of many of these jobs requires organizational skills that will allow you to retrieve information and redirect it to customers or coworkers at a moment's notice.

Although important, retrieval of information is rarely a matter of life and death in the business world. However, it very well could be in the profession of dispatcher, which we cover in this volume. Although dispatchers can be vital for the commercial success of delivery, repair, or taxi companies, or even your local transit authority, dispatchers engaged in the exciting field of public safety (police, fire, ambulance) have to keep track of the whereabouts of their departments' vehicles at all times so they can quickly answer calls for help from the general public that may truly be a matter of life and death.

As much as it's important to underscore what you're doing from day to day, how you do your job may be just as important in determining your career success. Whether you're working behind the counter of a bank, in a call center station, on the floor of a retail department store, or in the reception area of a business, the value of how you conduct yourself and the impression you make on others should not be underestimated.

In addition to being information managers, many professionals in the fields we'll cover are vital in helping make a first impression to a potential client or customer. It's important to remember that the quality of a business and sales relationship can depend heavily and the quality of the experience a client or customer has while interacting with you and your company.

Is a Retail, Sales, or Finance Career Right for You?

Ask yourself the following questions to see if the careers in this book might be right for you.

- ✴ Can I be patient with customers?
- ✴ Am I comfortable with handling money and making change?
- ✴ Are viewpoints of other people easy to see?

✴ Can I help people find what they want?

✴ Do I have solid attention to detail?

✴ Can I stand on my feet for long periods of time?

✴ Am I OK with performing repetitive tasks accurately?

✴ Do I have strong organizational skills?

✴ Am I comfortable in dealing with members of the general public?

✴ Do I enjoy working with computers?

✴ Can I be trusted with confidential information?

✴ Am I good at working unsupervised for extended periods of time?

✴ Will I be flexible about my work schedule?

✴ Do I enjoy business?

✴ Can I get along with different personalities?

✴ Can others rely on me?

✴ Am I a team player who can take directions from others?

✴ Can I handle pressure?

✴ Am I a quick thinker?

If you answered "Yes" to most of these, then a retail, sales, or finance career might be for you.

Learn the Skills

Typically, when people think about the retail, finance, or sales professions, many make the false assumption that most jobs require some formal business education. And while it's true that stockbrokers, bank vice presidents, account managers, and similar professionals require advanced degrees, many rewarding retail, finance, or sales careers are available to high school graduates.

The fact of the matter is, you don't need a business degree to step firmly into the vocational business ventures we'll present in this volume. An aspiring professional in any of these fields has to know how to think quickly on his or her feet. A secretary has to know the roles of all who work in his or her organization and how to reroute vital information to the appropriate party in a timely matter, while a customer service representative or telemarketer may have to retrieve information at a moment's notice to help retain a customer or effectively close the deal on making a sale.

Certainly, some jobs of interest to high school graduates ask for a bit more preparation in the form of specialized training. To work as a legal or medical secretary requires training to help learn the concepts, terms, and practices specific to the profession. Anyone working the field of financial collections or payroll may wish to seek out certification training to become more marketable for advancement.

More important, many of these jobs are open to high school graduates with a willingness to learn new skills. In this volume, you'll learn about the many rewarding career opportunities for high school graduates. The training requirements will vary, depending on the job and the employer. In some retail or office settings, for example, you may be able to start working right out of high school and will receive your training on the job. In many cases, if you want to get a leg up on the competition in terms of preparation, you needn't look any further than your high school. For some of the financial services jobs, such as bank teller or account collector, enrolling in an accounting class will give you the basics you'll need to feel confident during the interview process or during your first day on the job. For those drawn to join an office setting as a secretary or administrative assistant, time invested in a typing class or typing instructional CD-ROM would be time well spent. So, develop your skills, and check out any career fairs your high school or other area institutions may have. Explore with an open mind to find if a particular field is right for you.

While in high school, you can start laying the foundation to help you prepare for a business career. To get off on the right foot, enrolling in accounting, basic computer courses, and communication classes will help you gain the skills you need to successfully calculate sales, retrieve information, or communicate effectively with your coworkers and customers. And if you have the chance for an interesting volunteer position, or even to do some light retail hours to get a feel for things, such experiences can only inform you and boost your credibility as an applicant later. Who knows? You may even make professional contacts in your field, which can often play a pivotal role in finding a permanent position after you've finished high school. And when you know a good bit about what you want to do, you are in a good position to learn from those around you. Reading this book is a great step toward paving your way to a bright future.

Master office technology

Secretary/ Administrative Assistant/ Receptionist

Keep operations running smoothly

Coordinate communications

Secretary/Administrative Assistant/Receptionist

The job description for administrative assistant lies somewhere between corporate ambassador and intelligent octopus. These office professionals—sometimes working under the title of "secretary" or "receptionist"—juggle various duties from word processing to filing documents to fielding phone calls. Their jobs have become more sophisticated as the workplace has expanded its technological capabilities. Businesses depend on administrative assistants to keep operations running smoothly. Secretaries often coordinate all the administrative activities in an office, making sure information and messages are efficiently stored and delivered. As a company's ambassador, the assistant is frequently the first representative that a visitor will meet, so he or she must have a neat appearance, pleasant personality, strong communications skills, and a thorough knowledge of operations. Today there are about 5.2 million jobs in the field, and new positions are growing, according to 2006 figures from the U.S. Bureau of Labor Statistics. Physicians' offices, law firms, and traditional businesses depend on administrative support and the daily handling of clerical and interpersonal tasks to keep running smoothly. Demand is highest for office professionals who know their way around software applications or those who specialize in the legal or medical field.

Is This Job for You?

To find out if being an administrative assistant is a good fit for you, read each of the following questions and answer "Yes" or "No."

Yes	No	**1.**	Are you capable of doing two or more things at once?
Yes	No	**2.**	Are you good at prioritizing tasks and work?
Yes	No	**3.**	Can you take direction well?
Yes	No	**4.**	Are you comfortable with computers and software basics (Word, Excel, Outlook, PowerPoint)?
Yes	No	**5.**	Are you a detail-oriented person?
Yes	No	**6.**	Do organizational skills come naturally to you?
Yes	No	**7.**	Can you perform repetitive tasks with accuracy?

Let's Talk Money

Secretary and administrative assistant wages average $16.81 an hour in the United States, according to 2006 data from the Bureau of Labor Statistics. Depending on whether you work for the government, businesses, or schools, pay can range between $11.37 and $18.72 per hour. According to the bureau, secretaries and administrative assistants earn on average $34,970 per year with the top 10 percent earning more than $53,460. Receptionists make on average $10.50 per hour, or about $21,800 per year. Receptionists employed by the federal government earn a higher wage, typically earning more than $29,000 per year.

Yes *No* **8.** Do you work well with others?

Yes *No* **9.** Can you present yourself in a manner that reflects the image of the company?

Yes *No* **10.** Do you have good typing and filing skills?

If you answered "Yes" to most of these questions, consider a career as a secretary, administrative assistant, or receptionist. To find out more about these jobs, read on.

What You'll Do

As a professional in this field, your work will play a key role in the day-to-day operations that keep businesses, schools, hospitals, and other organizations running smoothly. With computers and the Internet becoming indispensable parts of our everyday lives, the traditional secretary and assistant who once took dictation now conducts research on the Internet and helps troubleshoot new office technologies.

This job is much more than just word processing. Whether the position is at General Electric, the U.S. Department of Agriculture, or the elementary school around the corner, careers in this field revolve around the processing and organization of information. As the nerve center of a business, school, or other locale, you will absorb information and develop a solid overview of how your business works. Organization is the name of the game. Not only will you need to be organized, but you must keep everybody else coordinated and on schedule as you call to arrange meetings and appointments for office staff. Depending on the profession you're supporting, your administrative tasks may also include processing mail, and handling travel or guest arrangements.

The majority of the work you do will not be physically demanding, but it will be mentally challenging to keep track of many conversations, people, computer files, and other bits of information all at once. Although you'll be on your feet from time to time using photocopiers or even making the odd trip to Kinko's, the physical challenge may result from prolonged work with your keyboard. Eyestrain and carpal tunnel syndrome are common ailments for secretaries and administrative assistants. If possible, break up your workday to include a full range of responsibilities so you won't have to do too much of one thing repeatedly.

Who You'll Work For

- ✴ Small and large businesses
- ✴ Elementary, junior, or senior high schools—both public and private
- ✴ Law firms
- ✴ Health organizations, including hospitals and private practices
- ✴ Government agencies
- ✴ Community colleges or universities
- ✴ Construction companies
- ✴ Media companies

Let's Talk Trends

Secretaries, administrative assistants, and receptionists are always in demand. According to the Bureau of Labor Statistics, the field should add an average of 50,000 jobs per year through 2014. Yesterday, today, and tomorrow, secretaries and administrative assistants have been and will be one of largest parts of the American workforce. Strong areas of growth are in health care and legal services, as well as scientific and technical services.

Where You'll Work

Although you may think of this work as mostly taking place in large office buildings, secretaries are needed in schools, hospitals, and government agencies as well as legal and medical offices. According to the U.S. Department of Labor, out of the 4.1 million secretary or administrative assistant jobs, a sizable fraction specialize as medical and legal secretaries.

As a professional in this field, you typically work at a desk in front of a computer monitor. Most of your time on the job is spent sitting, but you occasionally spring into motion to handle fax machines, photocopiers, and scanning equipment. If you work as a receptionist in a service industry such as a beauty or hair salon, your duties will include setting up appointments, directing customers, and serving as a cashier.

Hours in this field are typically a standard 40-hour workweek, although nearly one in five secretaries work in a part-time capacity, with a smaller percentage participating in job-sharing arrangements where a single job is divided up between two people.

Your Typical Day

Here are the highlights of a typical day at an office setting as an administrative assistant.

✔ **Check equipment.** Make a swing past the fax machine to see if there are any arriving documents that need to be passed along. Check your voicemail to check for either cancellations or reconfirmations of appointments. It's not a bad idea to see if the copier is working and that it has the toner it needs; after all, it's likely you'll need it later.

✔ **Take care of communications.** Depending on the size of your organization, you will spend a lot of time routing phone calls, e-mails, and written correspondence to the appropriate party. As new information comes in, you may be asked to compose letters, create spreadsheets, or manage databases.

✔ **Greet visitors.** You are the first impression for most visitors, so you have to maintain a professional appearance and be ready to communicate with others in a courteous manner.

✔ **Type and file.** A good portion of your day is devoted to filing documents and typing letters and other information.

✔ **Stay on your toes and keep learning.** If there's a break in the day, take a moment to learn how to put together a presentation in Power-Point, one of the Microsoft Office suite's applications, or learn how the company's videoconferencing system works. Greater responsibility and challenging work will follow if you demonstrate your interest to take on new things.

✔ **Maintain supplies.** Review inventory to make sure that you have all the little items you need to keep business churning. It's hard to make copies, print presentations, or receive faxes if you're out of toner or paper.

What You Can Do Now

✴ Look for an after-school or summer job that will give you a chance to increase your exposure to an office environment. If you're having a hard time getting started, consider taking on a part-time position as a volunteer at a religious or community center—they're always looking for a helping hand.

✴ Brush up on your typing skills.

✴ Consider a specialized training program if you're interested in becoming a medical or legal secretary.

✴ See if your high school offers typing or computer skills classes. If your school has a computer lab, spend some time getting familiar with Internet search engines such as Google and Yahoo!

What Training You'll Need

If you're a high school graduate with basic office skills, you should be able to get started pretty quickly. Receptionists should be comfortable greeting people and spending a lot of time on the phone, while secretaries and administrative assistants should possess good typing skills in addition to an eagle eye for spelling, punctuation, and grammar. Regardless of field or specialty, the way an organization stores and retrieves information can change with the season, so some of the training you'll need in the latest office technology may come in the form of either enrollment in an online class or by attending a seminar. Software packages for businesses are updating all the time; it'll be part of your job to keep up. If you can showcase your stellar interpersonal and organizational skills and can demonstrate at least some familiarity with office technology, your employer will likely be happy

The Inside Scoop: Q&A

Antoinette Smith, CPS/CAP (certified professional secretary/certified administrative professional)
Executive office administrator
St. Louis, Missouri

Q: *How did you get your job?*

A: Creating a career portfolio and using it during my interview helped me to get the position in my current assignment. I was interviewed by a panel, and I went into the interview equipped with my portfolio and showed samples of successful projects I had completed along with statements from internal and external customers describing my performance. That same day I was offered the position. I was told that all the candidates brought similar experience and skill sets as mine, but the panel was very impressed with the preparation I had taken with my portfolio for the interview. Very few administrative assistants were using portfolios at that time, and it gave me an edge. Taking extra steps to prepare for the interview was a key factor as they made a short list of potential hires—and I was the candidate selected for the job.

Q: *What's the most challenging part of your job?*

A: A challenging part of my job is also what I love about my job and that is managing multiple bosses. The challenge is servicing all of them as a priority and then prioritizing the priorities.

Q: *What do you like best about your job?*

A: I love the variety of things I do in my job—managing multiple projects and bosses and being the key "go-to" person for policies and procedures as well assisting others with the day-to-day operations of the office.

Q: *What are the keys to success to being an administrative professional?*

A: To achieve success as an administrative assistant, you need to be dependable, flexible, and adaptable. You must accept changes in

(Continued on next page)

(continued from previous page)

technology, people, and job responsibilities. In addition, good communication skills (listening, spoken, written, and body language), a good attitude, a commitment to continuous learning, and working with integrity are musts for being successful.

to show you the rest. Every business is different, and knowing that, most employers are quick to provide the on-the-job training necessary to make you a vital part of the organization. Many of the office computer skills you may need are also available at temporary placement agencies. If you just want to dip your toe in the pool rather than dive in head first, a short temping assignment could give you exposure to the technological tools you're likely to need.

If you have your heart set on working in the medical or legal field, specialized programs are available for anyone interested in becoming a medical or legal secretary. Some assistants advance by earning certification as a CPS/CAP (certified professional secretary/certified administrative professional). Accounting skills and fluency in a foreign language can also open doors to more challenging positions.

How to Talk Like a Pro

Here are a few words you'll hear as a secretary, administrative assistant or receptionist:

- **Bookkeeping** The recording of all financial transactions.
- **Dictation** Taking notes of someone speaking.
- **Shorthand** An abbreviated writing method used for taking dictation. Employing a system of symbols or abbreviations for words and frequently used phrases, effective use of shorthand allows someone to write as quickly as they are being spoken to.
- **Transcribe** To make a typed copy from handwritten notes or a recorded tape.

How to Find a Job

There isn't a sector of the working world that isn't supported by secretaries, receptionists, or administrative assistants. If there's a particular business or industry that captures your interest, try using a keyword search. Just hop onto Google or Yahoo!, type in the industry in which you're interested and any or all of the positions we've described in this chapter.

Often, a temping agency may be the best place to start, particularly if you need to sharpen your computer skills. Temp agencies or staffing agencies are listed in the Yellow Pages; all you need to do is pick up the phone and make an appointment. Many of these agencies provide tutorials on all the Microsoft basics you'll need to succeed in an office environment. Based on your strengths, you could be assigned to a company for anywhere from a week to three months. The fact is, many businesses hire permanent secretaries and office help from temping agencies. This gives them a chance to see who you are and gives you an opportunity to see if this particular work environment agrees with you. As you take on other assignments, you'll have a chance to pick up additional office computer skills and receive lengthier assignments that could turn into full-time positions. Of course, finding a job may be just as simple as submitting a résumé online and making a good impression at your interview, but if you think you need more experience, starting out at a temp agency could be your first big step in this career.

Cliché as it may sound, it doesn't hurt to dress for success. Before going in for an interview or before you drop off that résumé, do a little research by visiting a place similar to the place to which you wish to apply. Of course, how you should dress depends on where you want to work. A nose piercing and blue hair won't get you far in a traditional office setting; however, if you have your sights set on a receptionist job with a hair salon—that could be just the thing.

Secrets for Success

See the following suggestions and turn to the appendix for advice on résumés and interviews.

- ✴ Analyze and prioritize. When the phone starts to ring and visitors start to pile up, it's easy to lose sight of deadlines and lose contact with those who depend on you for appointment reminders, documents and other forms of support. Making a plan may sound simple, but it becomes more of a challenge to stick to if you're asked (and you will be) to do two things at once.
- ✴ Improve velocity and accuracy of typing skills. Your proficiency will free up your day to attend to other tasks.

Reality Check

Spend a day inside answering e-mails and organizing all your paperwork—bills, taxes, old homework, photos. If you enjoy the process of getting things in order, administrative work could be for you.

Some Other Jobs to Think About

⭐ Legal secretary. Legal secretaries perform specialized work requiring knowledge of technical procedures and terms. Under the supervision of an attorney, legal secretaries prepare correspondence and legal papers such as summonses, complaints, motions, responses, and subpoenas.

⭐ Medical secretary. Medical secretaries are similar to their legal counterparts in terms of specialization, but are more likely to transcribe dictation. In addition to achieving familiarity with insurance rules, billing practices, and hospital procedures, medical secretaries also assist physicians or medical scientists with speeches, reports, articles and conference proceedings.

How You Can Move Up

⭐ Become an office manager. Use your organizational skills to make the purchasing and hiring decisions that keep an office running.

⭐ Earn credentials as a certified administrative professional. You can earn this designation through study and passing an exam, thereby increasing your prospects for becoming an executive secretary or executive administrative assistant.

⭐ Become a paralegal. With some additional training, many legal secretaries go on to become paralegals, helping attorneys conduct research and manage the daily tasks for cases.

⭐ Get two-year training. Many vo-tech and community colleges offer one or two-year office administration programs. Once you've got your foot in the door and you've decided that you want to stay and move up, acquiring some additional skills could get you to that next level and/or next pay grade.

Web Sites to Surf

The Association of Executive and Adminstrative Professionals. Established in 1975, the association provides a job bank and home study courses to help professionals sharpen their administrative and secretarial skills. http://www.theaeap.com

National Association for Legal Secretaries. With chapters nationwide, the association offers online learning opportunities and professional growth seminars geared toward educating and helping people become certified legal professionals.   http://www.nals.org

Defend the bottom line

Financial Clerk/ Bookkeeper

Master the science of managing money

Work at the heart of your company

Financial Clerk/Bookkeeper

Let's face it, the world depends on clerks. Without the billing and customer support these professionals provide, goods would remain unshipped, employees and bills would go unpaid. Government agencies, hospitals, and retail establishments would collapse and anarchy would soon follow. Clerks keep track of requests for materials or money—the two elements you need for creating and staying in business. Today more than 600,000 financial clerks are employed in the United States, according to the U.S. Bureau of Labor Statistics, and the demand for these financial professionals continues. Although it's true that automation and the Internet have eliminated the mailing of some paper bills, invoices still must be calculated, and organizations depend on professionals to help field billing questions from customers, suppliers, and even government agencies. As the health care industry continues to grow, the demand for billing clerks in the specialized medical field will rise. This adds up to a field with a healthy employment outlook. With some basic math and office skills and a little on-the-job training to learn billing software, you could make a successful leap into this vital occupation.

Is This Job for You?

To find out if being a financial clerk is a good fit for you, read each of the following questions and answer "Yes" or "No."

Yes   No   **1.** Can you perform the same task several times without sacrificing accuracy?

Yes   No   **2.** Do you like working with the general public and would you be happy to help answer questions or concerns from customers?

Yes   No   **3.** Can you be trusted with confidential information?

Yes   No   **4.** Are you comfortable with computers and software basics?

Yes   No   **5.** Do you enjoy working with numbers?

Yes   No   **6.** Do you pay close attention to details?

Yes   No   **7.** Do you trust yourself to spot an error and to take the steps needed to correct it?

Yes   No   **8.** Are you comfortable with learning how to use new computer software?

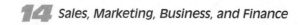

Let's Talk Money

Wages for financial clerks vary as much by region as they do by profession. Billing clerks earned an average of $13.00 per hour, with an annual salary of $27,000, with the highest 10 percent earning more than $39,270 per year, according to 2006 data from the Bureau of Labor Statistics. Payroll clerks, on the other hand, garnered an average wage of $14.60 per hour, making a yearly salary of more than $30,000. The highest 10 percent earned more than $44,200 per year. According to the bureau, earnings for purchasing or procurement clerks clocked in at an hourly wage of $14.85, or nearly $31,000 per year. Purchasing clerks working for the federal government earned an average annual income of $39,000, while, according to Salary.com, medical billing clerks brought home a yearly salary of around $30,000.

Yes   No   **9.**   Can you work unsupervised for long periods of time?

Yes   No   **10.**   Do you possess a knack for staying organized?

If you answered "Yes" to most of these questions, consider a career as a financial, payroll, purchasing, or billing clerk. To find out more about these jobs, read on.

What You'll Do

As a financial clerk working either in payroll, purchasing, or billing, your job could involve calculating wages or bills, working with fellow employees and customers, or ordering goods and supplies, all in an effort to ensure that your organization functions smoothly. It sounds simple enough, but if you're not well organized the job can get out of hand quickly as the papers start to pile up. Billing clerks compile records of charges, calculating and recording the amounts of goods sold or services provided. Although it is rather straightforward to write up a line-by-line description to inform a customer of how much they owe for a pair of concert tickets or pile of V-neck sweaters, billing can be a far more intricate undertaking. For example, an employee in the retail field will need to incorporate applicable discounts or terms of credit. If you work for a trucking company, you'll spend a good part of your day thumbing through a trusty rate book to help determine the shipping cost for the 500 pounds of widgets you need to send to Walla Walla by Wednesday. What you do, of course, will be largely determined by where you work. If you work at a physician's office or a hospital, your medical billing clerk duties typically include contacting insurance companies or state aid agencies to determine which physicians or patients can be reimbursed and for how much. If you work as a billing clerk in the legal or financial services sector, it will be your job to keep track of the work provided while working out how much to charge for each job and making a note of how much of the job still needs to be completed.

Whatever your clerking role is, you'll need to be good with numbers. You won't need to solve for the right angle of a hypotenuse (unless you're shipping triangles to a geometry teacher), but you will need to be comfortable with computers. These days, specialized billing software allows clerks to calculate charges and prepare bills in one fell swoop. While producing invoices requires attention to detail and a solid grasp of math basics, some billing clerks also handle follow-up questions from customers, which could include resolving any billing errors or questions about a particular charge. All clerk jobs provide an education in how organizations function and stay in business—your ability to calculate fees and keep track of records will play an essential role in keeping your business running.

Who You'll Work For

✳ Health care firms
✳ Third-party billing companies
✳ Accounting firms

Let's Talk Trends

Payroll and billing clerks are in demand. New positions are opening all the time as established clerks gain certification and move on to higher positions. According to 2006 figures from the Bureau of Labor Statistics, purchasing, or procurement, clerks held 74,000 positions, with three in 10 working for state, local, or federal governments. Medical billing clerks account for about one job in three in this field of more than 600,000 jobs.

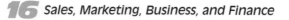

* Tax-preparation firms
* Federal, state, local governments
* Manufacturing (purchasing clerk)
* Retail and wholesale trade

Where You'll Work

One of the wonderful things about being a billing clerk is that it offers workplace flexibility. Although a traditional office setting is typical for most billing clerks, according to the U.S. Department of Labor, an increasing number of medical billing clerks are punching their clock from home. Work locations could include a skyscraper, an office park, or a physician's office in a medical building across the street from a hospital. If you can develop a strong enough reputation for efficiency and accuracy, there's a chance you may go into business for yourself. According to the Bureau of Labor Statistics, 3 percent of medical billers are self-employed. Typically, clerks put in 40-hour workweeks, although payroll clerks may put in longer workweeks when timesheets have been handed in and paychecks need to be calculated.

Your Typical Day

Here are the highlights of a typical day as a financial, payroll, purchasing, or billing clerk.

✔ **Call in and then track your orders.** If you're a purchasing clerk, chances are you'll be busy ordering the goods and supplies that keep your organization running. It will also be up to you to make sure that what you ordered matches the purchaser's needs and arrives on schedule.

✔ **Calculate charges.** If you're a billing clerk, you'll need to dig into those on-screen computer forms and start calculating who owes how much and to whom. In addition to calculating billing charges, you'll assign numbers to packages or accounts for the purpose of tracking a package or shipment.

✔ **Process time cards.** If you're a payroll clerk, you'll process time cards and deal with everybody's wages, salaries, and withholdings. Your ability to pay everyone correctly and keep tight-lipped on what everybody makes will go a long way to earning the respect of your coworkers.

The Inside Scoop: Q&A

Larry White
Director of payroll training
San Antonio, Texas

Q: *How did you get your job?*

A: Three little words propelled me into a profession
I've enjoyed for 26 years. Like many payroll professionals, I was asked by my supervisor to step into an unfamiliar
position following the resignation of my company's payroll manager. My answer? "Yes, I will." With no more payroll experience
than getting a paycheck every other week, I managed to pick up
information wherever I could to make sure the employees at my
firm were paid accurately and on time every payday.

Q: *What do you like best about your job?*

A: Giving away money. It's my job—it's why people go to work. It's
a goal-oriented profession not unlike professional sports. Just like
an NFL quarterback prepares for his next game, I prepare for the
next payday. When the paychecks are distributed and the employees are happy, it's just like I've scored the winning touchdown.

Q: *What's the most challenging part of your job?*

A: The two biggest challenges I face every day are keeping my company in compliance with federal and state regulations and making sure employees are paid accurately and on time. Everything
revolves around those two concerns. A payroll department may
not be an earning component of a corporation, but ensuring a
company's compliance with constantly changing federal and state
laws is crucial to the success of any business. For example, helping a company avoid being hit by a $1 million penalty from the
Internal Revenue Service or U.S. Department of Labor can certainly affect the company's financial bottom line. The challenge
in paying employees lies more in what's taken away than what's
earned. Taxation and deductions demand the most attention
when it comes to calculating an employee's paycheck. The wide

(Continued on next page)

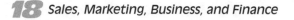

(continued from previous page)

variety of benefits and tax-savings options available for employees as a deduction from their paycheck typically leads to a parade of compliance issues.

Q: *What are the keys to success to being a payroll clerk?*

A: Knowledge, patience, and an unquenchable passion to get things right are the prime ingredients in a successful payroll career. Since you won't find an undergraduate degree in payroll administration in any university curriculum, most payroll professionals obtain knowledge through experience and continuing education from industry organizations like ours.

Payroll certifications offered by the American Payroll Association can also help payroll professionals prove their knowledge of payroll to current and future employers. Patience is not only a virtue but also a necessity. By pure ratio, megacorporations may be supported by only a small group of payroll professionals. In many small companies, a single employee may handle all of the company's payroll responsibilities. Successful payroll professionals all have one thing in common—passion for their work. Getting paid correctly is the right of every worker in America, and payroll professionals are passionate about ensuring every employee gets paid correctly and on time.

✔ **Turn that medical mountain into a molehill.** Physicians are flooded with insurance paperwork these days. If you work as a medical billing clerk, your job will be to process medical claims, handle patient invoices, and track down reimbursement for both patients and doctors. If you can get a real handle on this job, you may be able to start your own business from home with flexible hours.

What You Can Do Now

✯ Look for a course or program in accounting at your high school or local business college. Get a head start on learning how to execute such business fundamentals as calculating, deducting, and getting your accounts to balance.

✯ Volunteer at any setting that's likely to offer you exposure to office equipment and computer software fundamentals such as the Microsoft Office suite programs Word and Excel.

✯ Take a typing class at high school, or check out a typing CD-ROM from your local library, or purchase one from your local bookstore. Those invoices aren't going to type themselves and the more comfortable with a keyboard you are, the more efficient you'll be.

✯ Enroll in a medical billing course.

✯ Create your own budget and stick with it. Tracking income and expenses with a logbook or computer spreadsheet can be part of this job.

What Training You'll Need

If you've got a firm grasp of numbers and know your way around computer basics such as Microsoft Word, Microsoft Excel, or Microsoft Office, you're well on your way to becoming a financial clerk. As is the case with payroll, purchasing, and billing clerks, most employees are taken under the supervision of a more experienced worker who will instruct you on the finer points of preparing a purchase order. Additionally, some financial clerks receive formal classroom training as they start to get their heads around billing software programs.

If you're interested in becoming a billing clerk in the potentially more flexible field of medical billing, you won't be able to just walk in the door and get started. You'll need to get a grasp on how the medical industry works in order to get hired or get ahead. You might be able to join a physician's office as a receptionist and gradually pick up medical billing procedures, but a little formal or informal training will take you a long way. Many online and local specialty colleges offer yearlong at-home courses to specifically train those who want to join the medical billing field.

How to Talk Like a Pro

Here are a few words you'll hear as a financial clerk:

✯ **Invoice** Taking the form of paper or email, invoices are a document issued by a seller to a buyer, indicating the product,

quantity and price for goods or services provided, usually listing a date when payment is due.

✦ **Health Insurance Portability and Accountability Act (HIPPA)** An indispensable part of medical billing, the federal law known by the
acronym "HIPAA" requires the adherence to national standards
for electronic health care transactions, the safeguarding of
patient information, and provides national identifiers for
providers, health insurance plans, and employers.

✦ **Timesheet** Used by payroll clerks to calculate paychecks,
timesheets let employees keep track of hours worked. They also
indicate work for hourly services as provided by employees or
outside help such as lawyers or consultants.

How to Find a Job

Many different businesses hire financial clerks, so take a look around
for operations that may best suit you. Are there hospitals, government
agencies, or tax preparation firms near you? If you've received payroll
certification or graduated from a medical billing course, you'll have a
leg up on your competition. Certification or course completion isn't always a requirement and many employers will either provide training
or help you get certified. Many federal employees start out at the local
or state level. If you want to start applying immediately, just go to an
Internet search engine or job page, which could include Career-
Builder, Yahoo!, and Monster.com. Just select your part of the country
and type in any of the different types of clerks we've discussed in the
chapter. If you're interested in becoming a payroll clerk, you may want
to see if one of Accountemps' 330 worldwide offices is somewhere near
you. Visit http://www.accountemps.com for more details.

Secrets for Success

See the following suggestions and turn to the appendix for advice on
résumés and interviews.

✦ Move those invoices, but make sure you move, too. Although
you'd expect eyestrain for a job that comes with a heavy dose of
numbers, the fact of the matter is that financial clerks do a lot of
repetitive motions while sitting and working at their keyboards.
Nip those backaches and headaches before they get started and
make sure you stretch your legs frequently.

✴ Double-check your work. This is a detail-oriented career and mistakes can be costly, so review your work carefully.

Reality Check

Although your job may seem simple enough at times as you write up bills or calculate paychecks, keep in mind that this is other people's money and finances you're dealing with. When digits are left off or added on, the resulting difference can be substantial, resulting in a phone call from a distressed fellow employee or customer. Can you stay calm and reassure an employee or customer that this the matter is important to you? You need to prove yourself as calm, trustworthy, and accurate to tackle this job.

Some Other Jobs to Think About

✴ Bill and account collector. Bill and account collectors perform tasks that are quite similar to billing clerks. Collectors are tasked with locating and notifying customers of delinquent accounts, usually over the telephone. You can read about this profession in greater detail in Chapter 5.

✴ Bookkeeping, auditing, or accounting clerk. Accounting for more than two million jobs nationwide, bookkeepers are similar to other financial clerks, except that they provide a broader line of services. Their duties are often similar to those of a payroll clerk, as they keep track of receipts and accounts payable and receivable, while also handling payroll, bank deposits, and invoices.

How You Can Move Up

✴ Become a purchasing agent or buyer. If you can put in a little time at your local business college and demonstrate a solid understanding of contracts and purchasing, you can advance to being a buyer or purchaser.

✴ Seek a billing supervisor position. Demonstrate your mastery of the billing software and the workings of the company. In this career, you may direct a team of billing clerks and report billing activity for your team. Now you're talking to management.

✴ Get certified. If you're a payroll clerk, you can demonstrate your commitment to your craft by obtaining fundamental payroll certification.

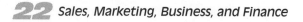

✷ Become an accountant. With some outside education or home study, you can build on your financial clerking expertise and become a professional who helps maintain and determine the financial health of an organization.

✷ Apply for a payroll manager spot. Dig in and learn about federal and state laws and see how they relate to the use of overtime and deductions. If you're at the top of the payroll heap, it'll be up to you to make sure your reports to the government are on time and accurate.

Web Sites to Surf

American Payroll Association. With a nationwide membership, the association offers audio seminars, payroll certification programs, and a career page offering tips on cover letters and handling interviews.
http://www.americanpayroll.org

American Purchasing Society. This site offers information for purchasing professionals, including details on how to earn certification as either a certified professional purchasing manager or certified purchasing professional.
http://www.american-purchasing.com

Deal with money

Bank Teller

Learn about the world of finance

Interact with customers

Bank Teller

If you're interested in learning more about the world of finance or banking but aren't sure if more schooling is the right path for you, consider a career as a bank teller at a commercial bank, savings institution, or credit union. As a bank teller, you will be a familiar face to many in your community as you help perform a major portion of your bank's activities. It's a job where you're constantly interacting with people and taking care of their personal and business banking needs. You deposit checks, handle withdrawals, and take care of loan payments. Beyond these basic transactions, you can learn about savings bonds, certificates of deposit (CDs) mortgages, and more sophisticated banking options. As your knowledge of banking grows, your opportunity to advance into positions of greater responsibility will, too.

Is This Job for You?

To find out if being a bank teller is a good fit for you, read each of the following questions and answer "Yes" or "No."

Yes	No	**1.**	Do you enjoy working with the general public?
Yes	No	**2.**	Are you a detail-oriented person?
Yes	No	**3.**	Can you stand on your feet for extended periods of time?
Yes	No	**4.**	Are you well organized?
Yes	No	**5.**	Do you possess strong basic math skills?
Yes	No	**6.**	Are you comfortable with computers and the Internet?
Yes	No	**7.**	Can you keep confidential information to yourself?
Yes	No	**8.**	Are you willing to work the occasional Saturday?
Yes	No	**9.**	Are you trustworthy and able to handle large amounts of money?
Yes	No	**10.**	Do you enjoy listening to and learning from supervisors and customers?

If you answered "Yes" to most of these questions, consider a career as a bank teller. To find out more about this job, read on.

Let's Talk Money

Bank teller wages average $10.15 per hour in the U.S., according to 2006 data from the U.S. Bureau of Labor Statistics. Where you live, however, could affect how much you earn, with hourly wages varying between $7.60 and $13.50 per hour. According to the bureau, bank tellers earn on average $21,000 per year, with the top 10 percent earning more than $28,000 annually.

What You'll Do

As a bank teller, you'll work on the frontlines of financial customer service. You serve as an ambassador for your institution as you help customers conduct routine and more detailed transactions. Beyond the standard cashing of checks and assisting with deposits, you may sell savings bonds, accept customer payments for utility bills, process paperwork for certificates of deposit, and sell traveler's checks. Depending on the size of the bank, some tellers specialize in handling commercial or business accounts, or in the handling of foreign currencies.

Solid math skills come into play on a daily basis, but for a successful bank teller, there is no substitute for excellent communication skills. Your ability to articulate bank procedures and services in a courteous manner is central to a bank's reputation. Precision is vital as you record financial figures. Mistakes regarding an individual's bank account can be costly to the customer and your bank. An extra zero here and there can mean big money and big headaches. That's why it's so important to review your work in this occupation. And you have to work fast. After all, customers often come in on work breaks and they need to take care of business in a hurry.

Who You'll Work For

* Commercial banks
* Savings institutions or credit unions
* Financial institutions where money is frequently exchanged—possibly brokerage firms and casinos

Let's Talk Trends

Today there are 560,000 bank tellers in the U.S., according to 2006 data from the Bureau of Labor Statistics, and employment prospects will continue to grow as banks build new branch offices as a way of attracting and enticing customers with new services and products. The rise of ATMs and computer banking, however, has eliminated some teller jobs, but as financial institutions compete to win and retain clients, they have expanded evening and weekend hours, which means more opportunities for tellers. Those who advance to manager level build a skill set that is applicable in many other retail settings. In a field where there is heavy turnover, opportunities to join and advance in banking are certainly there. Some banks offer a competitive benefits package including 401(k), profit sharing, and education reimbursement.

Where You'll Work

Typically, bank tellers ply their trade in a well-lit office environment. Your day-to-day environment is likely to include a mix of standing and sitting as you attend to your bank's most valuable asset—the customer. You might be in a newly built branch office of a well-known national bank or you could end up at a credit union serving the employees of only one company, such as Boeing. You will work as a team. You usually begin in a student capacity, learning the ropes of conducting bank procedures.

Like many customer service careers, your environment will be shaped by the rush hours and dead periods throughout the day. You can expect the lunch hour and the end of the day to be your busiest times. Your hours will typically be an eight-hour shift within the time frame of 7:30 a.m. to 8 p.m. Some days you may be asked to help open, while on others you'll arrive a little later and your workday will end by helping to close the bank. As banks seek new ways to retain customers, many are offering Saturday hours, so you may need to work the occasional Saturday.

The Inside Scoop: Q&A

Kate Robertson
Bank teller
Seattle, Washington

Q: *How did you get your job?*

A: I was barely making minimum wage at a coffee shop in Seattle, and this girl came in asking if anyone was interested in a new job with decent pay, health benefits, and education reimbursement. She gave me her card and told me to come talk to her after I got off work if I was interested. I did, and two weeks later I found myself in training to be a teller.

Q: *What do you like best about your job?*

A: By far the most enjoyable part of being a teller is interacting with tons of different people each day. I've learned a lot of really random things from our customers and have built many professional relationships based on their repeat visits. Money is a deeply personal and loaded subject. So, as a teller, we're on the frontline of an individual's financial interaction. We get to see a full range of emotion as they deal with what is or isn't going on in their account.

Q: *What's the most challenging part of your job?*

A: Monotony. Initially there is a learning curve and the first few months are exciting because there are so many rules and regulations of which to be aware. After settling down into the position, it can easily become boring because you are doing the same thing in and out, every day and very rarely come across new situations. Although banking offers room for growth, the growth is limited to the space available within the branch. So if you are working for an established team, it's difficult to take on new projects and grow, especially if your supervisor isn't supportive of that. Another thing that goes hand-in-hand with the monotony is that as tellers we're generally on the bottom of the ladder, so we often get stuck doing the tasks that no one else is willing to take on.

(Continued on next page)

(continued from previous page)

Q: *What are the keys to success to being a bank teller?*

A: Genuinely caring for customers sets apart a mediocre teller from an outstanding teller. The ability to look out for the best interest of a client is going to increase sales and allow you the grace to go the extra mile for the person in front of you—even if it's time consuming or not very interesting. Our position is to be the face of the bank and an access point for people who have genuine financial needs whether it is basic banking transactions, account issues, or new account referrals. So, caring for the customer is the first step to being a successful bank teller, everything else will grow from this.

Your Typical Day

Here are the highlights of a typical day at a financial institution as a bank teller.

✔ **Receive and count your money for your drawer.** Usually the head teller will verify your amount. Over the course of the day, you will be responsible for using this cash to pay customers, taking great care to be accurate.

✔ **Resolve out-of-balance passbooks with customers.** This happens when you and your client have different balances in your records. You will then need to work step-by-step with the customer to discover any mistakes that may have been made.

✔ **Say "Hello, how may I help you or direct your call?"** As you field phone or in-person inquiries about banking products, you will refer customers to the branch sales team.

✔ **Clerk 9-to-5, the way to make a living.** This could include typing, filing, answering the phone, and preparing check orders.

✔ **Bring balance to your day.** At the end of the day, you will balance your cash drawer and transactions to the teller system. If the amount of cash in the drawer agrees with your day's transaction records, you're set.

✔ **Identify the real and the fake.** Last but not least, you will keep an eye out for counterfeit bills and fake documents or signatures.

What You Can Do Now

* Look for a job opportunity that will give you experience in handling cash—a skill critical for being a good teller.
* Take math and business classes, including accounting—they will provide you with the fundamental numbers skills required for getting things to add up and balance out.
* Pay close attention to your own banking—keep careful track of deposits, withdrawals, interest earned, and terms used. Your personal banking concerns are often the concerns of a teller as well.
* Find a job rich in basic computer skills such as word processing and basic spreadsheet skills. A little knowledge of the Microsoft Office suite programs Word, Outlook, and Excel can go a long way.
* Banks are fundamentally about customer service. Any people-oriented experience you can pick up (and just as importantly employer references) will make you a more attractive job candidate.

What Training You'll Need

Nearly all tellers hold high school diplomas and have solid basic math skills. For those hiring from among prospective candidates, professional appearance, personality, and communication skills are the strongest of currencies. After all, it's your ability to interact with people that your customers, coworkers, and supervisor will remember. Although there are no state requirements for becoming a teller, applicants increase their chances of getting hired if they are already familiar with basic word processing and spreadsheet skills.

Once you've wowed them with your appearance and demonstrated that the calculator between your ears works properly, newly hired tellers can expect a steady diet of on-the-job training. Typically a supervisor or senior worker will take you under his or her wing and walk you through company procedures. This may include some classroom instruction at the corporate office or tutorial training in specific computer software. During your bank teller training, you'll learn how to interact with customers and resolve conflicts, sharpen your cash-handling skills, and learn how to process the transactions that are fundamental to the world of banking. If you work at a large bank, you can expect to receive at least one week of formal classroom

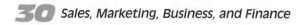

training. After you've demonstrated your ability to do your job, don't be shy in asking for more training. Tellers who can pick up new skills and broaden their knowledge base will ensure not only that their services are in demand but also that they will have a strong case for advancement and promotion.

How to Talk Like a Pro

Here are a few words you'll hear as a bank teller:

* **Time deposit** Also known as a CD, for "certificate of deposit," this term is used to describe money that is deposited at a banking institution that cannot be withdrawn for a certain period of time. These deposits typically produce a higher interest rate than regular savings accounts.
* **Overdraft** Hopefully you haven't heard this word too many times. This is the term used to describe when withdrawals from a bank account exceed the balance available to the customer. The result gives the account a negative balance, usually resulting in a fee to the customer.
* **Compound interest** This is interest calculated not only on the initial principal deposited but also on all the accumulated interest over prior periods.

How to Find a Job

To find a job, stop in at a branch of a bank and simply ask if they are looking for tellers. Chances are you may already know someone at your local bank by name; ask if they know any branch managers who are looking for more help. New positions open up frequently. Checking your local bank's Web site or even a job search engine (e.g., Monster.com) could provide you with a handful of fresh leads. Before you start to ask around about teller openings, however, it's a good idea to develop a sense of how the bank presents itself in the community. Take notes on how bank employees dress and present themselves. Your ability to make a good first impression as a professional and potential representative of the bank can go a long way to landing that first interview. While sharp threads and a solid grasp of numbers and computer basics will surely come in handy, you'll up your chances of getting hired if you declare your willingness to work weekends. Some banks require a minimum of two Saturdays a month.

Secrets for Success

See the following suggestions and turn to the appendix for advice on résumés and interviews.

- Keep your smile and patience. Can you handle the steady flow of customers? You have to stay pleasant even as the stream of people remains constant.
- Double-check your work. This is a detail-oriented job. It's more important to do it right than to do it quickly.
- Find a comfortable pair of shoes. Most of the time, you will be on your feet; you'll do your job better if you're not thinking about them.

Reality Check

Banking can be dirty business. Money is dirtier than it looks. Will you mind getting your hands soiled with dirty money? Plus, are you prepared to give up your early Friday evenings? Friday is often payday and banks often stay open late that night for their clientele.

Some Other Jobs to Think About

- Gaming cage worker. These workers draw from a similar set of skills as tellers. Those who work the "cage" operate in the casino's bank or depository, handling transactions for gaming chips, money, and the paperwork necessary for supporting casino play.
- Brokerage clerk. A crucial part of the financial world, brokerage clerks spend their days computing and recording securities transactions. Still in the field of customer service, brokerage clerks are frequently tasked with contacting customers, taking orders, and informing clients of changes to their account.

How You Can Move Up

- Become a head teller. Head tellers act as mentors and troubleshooters for more detailed problems. In addition to setting work schedules and ensuring that others follow bank procedures, head tellers oversee large cash transactions and ensure that the vault's cash balance is correct.

✦ Take courses offered by private financial institutions or local colleges. If you want to be promoted up the ladder, some additional training could make all the difference.

Web Sites to Surf

Bank Administration Institute. The institute is a leading professional organization designed to improve and enhance employee and bank performance. It publishes a monthly newsletter and offers education and training opportunities for those wishing to advance in their careers. http://www.bai.org

American Bankers Association. Established in 1875, the association represents the banking community in our nation's capital, offering resources to help educate and train members in the banking community. Complete with a lengthy list of banking topics for keeping tellers up-to-date, the site also offers a job bank. http://www.aba.com

Ensure accuracy in documentation

WordProcessor/
Data Entry
Worker

Maintain corporate communications

Learn businesses operations

Word Processor/Data Entry Worker

Printed documents—they're everywhere. Faxes, letters, reports, notes on meetings, data-filled spreadsheets. At first glance, they may just look like sheets of paper, but in fact these documents are critical to the everyday health of almost every organization, and they certainly didn't type or create themselves. Enter the world of the word processor and data-entry worker. There is a lot of overlap in these two career categories, but basically word processors do more straightforward typing of documents, while data entry workers key in figures and lists of items into spreadsheets and other forms.

These professionals are the unsung heroes of the workplace, whose fast finger work and accuracy is vital to churning out communications and records needed to maintain operations. About 525,000 information processors work in every part of the economy and new positions are opening daily, according to 2006 data from U.S. Bureau of Labor Statistics. Those who can develop a command in certain software applications and stay current with the latest technological developments will find even more opportunities. It's not rocket science. It's not even computer science. The career, however, is well suited for those with a passion for precision, punctuation, and communication. Almost all that you need to get started is a personal computer equipped with the standard keyboard and mouse and a commitment to learning the art of high-speed typing.

Is This Job for You?

To find out if being a word processor or data entry worker is a good fit for you, read each of the following questions and answer "Yes" or "No."

Yes	No	1.	Are you comfortable with a computer keyboard?
Yes	No	2.	Can you work quickly and accurately?
Yes	No	3.	Can you type at least 40 words per minute?
Yes	No	4.	Are you comfortable with computers and software basics (such as Microsoft Office suite programs Word and Excel)?
Yes	No	5.	Can you do repetitive tasks and do them accurately?
Yes	No	6.	Are you comfortable with a fast-paced environment?
Yes	No	7.	Can you prioritize tasks?

Let's Talk Money

Word processor wages average $13.47 per hour in the United States, earning an annual salary of $28,000 per year, according to 2006 data from the Bureau of Labor Statistics. The highest 10 percent made more than $43,000 per year. Those working for legal services typically made 25 percent more than other word processing professionals. Data entry wages average $11.17 per hour, earning an average salary of $23,250 per year. The highest 10 percent earned $28,150 per year, with employees in the insurance and accounting fields earning 10 percent more than other data processing jobs.

Yes	No	**8.**	Can you take direction well from others?
Yes	No	**9.**	Are you capable of doing two things at once?
Yes	No	**10.**	Can you sit for long periods of time?

If you answered "Yes" to most of these questions, consider a career as a word processor or data entry worker. To find out more about these jobs, read on.

What You'll Do

As a professional in this field, you'll help handle and process information that is effectively the lifeblood of an organization or business. You will key in text and enter data into a computer while also performing other office duties including filing, faxing, and photocopying documents. In the field of processing words, you may be asked to type up reports, letters, mailing labels, or even the occasional thank-you note. Sometimes, you may be transcribing from prerecorded tapes or from dictated notes. (Some businesses and government offices have a word processing team whose function centers almost exclusively around providing transcripts.) After you get in the door and dig out your coffee mug on the first day, your beginning tasks could include preparing company forms on computers, addressing letters, or keying in headings on form letters. Once you master the basics and prove yourself a stickler for details, you typically take on more intricate work. These tasks could include combining materials from different documents, planning statistical tables, or editing specialized technical material.

Whereas word processors pay close attention to words, data entry clerks deal more often in numbers. Workers in data entry typically input lists of items, numbers, or other information into computers, frequently completing forms on a computer screen. Types of information in this field that may be processed include customer information, medical records, or membership lists.

The work you do will require careful attention to detail, so you'll need to be alert. Word processors should be able to type a minimum of 40 words per minute. You'll also need to be able to organize information well, learn company or agency procedures, and stay current with office software applications. As you master all of these skills and office procedures, you will become more essential to an organization and able to advance to positions requiring greater management skills and responsibility. For example, Lyn Harris at the Ritz-Carlton hotel chain started out as a company typist but used the position as a stepping-stone toward becoming director of training and development.

Who You'll Work For

- ✶ Local or state governments
- ✶ Elementary and secondary schools
- ✶ Insurance companies
- ✶ Tax preparation, bookkeeping, or payroll services
- ✶ Legal services
- ✶ Temporary agencies

Where You'll Work

Have you ever seen the hit television show *The Office*? As an information processor, you're likely to star in an office setting as you help

Let's Talk Trends

Businesses, government agencies, and temporary staffing firms are always on the lookout for word processors and data entry clerks. Openings are produced each year as agencies expand and other workers transfer to more advanced positions. According to 2006 Bureau of Labor Statistics data, opportunities will be most plentiful for those with the best technical skills.

create the documents that play an essential role in the day-to-day operations of businesses and local organizations. You might work in a new, state-of-the-art office high atop the city, or you could be a part of a government bureau or an industrial office park that stretches as far as the eye can see. Local schools, hospitals, law offices, and more all need information processors, poised at their computer terminals, ready to type the day away.

Traditionally, data entry clerks and word processors work a standard 40-hour week in an office, often residing in cubicles in close proximity to various office machines (fax, photocopier, and coffee maker). According to the U.S. Department of Labor, approximately one in five data entry clerks and word processors held jobs in temporary agencies while another one in five worked for state or local governments.

Your Typical Day

Here are the highlights of a typical day at an office setting as either a word processor or data entry clerk.

✔ **Become one with your keyboard.** Keystrokes are the name of the game here. Upon arrival, you could have mini-cassette tapes that need to be transformed from dictations into written documents. Your keyboard duties could also include revising letters or adding additional information to a report or presentation.

✔ **Keep good form.** If you're working in data entry, you will likely have computer printouts of numbers or names needing to be entered into spreadsheets or standard company/agency forms.

✔ **Check to see if the mail has arrived.** Many word processors and data entry clerks are in charge of distributing mail. It's a good opportunity to stretch your legs and learn who your coworkers are.

✔ **Letters—lots and lots of letters to file.** Although much of your job will center on information creation, part of your job will depend upon information management. It will be up to you to file correspondence, reports, and even tapes and computer disks in an organized way that will allow you to retrieve them later at a moment's notice.

✔ **Stick to the format.** For word processors, you may be asked to handle many different formats for presenting information. Margins and spacing are essential for providing documents with a professional flair. It may not seem like much at first, but learning how to set margins, spacing, and tabs are a critical component of your job. (If you're using Microsoft Word, click on the "Format" portion of the menu at the top of the screen and select "Paragraph" to get some experience with this vital part of document preparation.) Toward the end of a day that isn't laden with heavy deadlines, you may spend 20 minutes brushing up your knowledge of the software commands.

What You Can Do Now

✯ If you're still in high school, get yourself into a basic computer skills class. Your exposure to Microsoft programs such as Word, Office, Excel, or Access will provide a foundation for future word processing or data entry tasks.

✯ Learn the hardware and peripherals. The more you know about the actual monitors, hard drives, printers, etc., the more employable you will be.

✯ Stop by a temporary work agency. Temp agencies, as they're known, are hungry to assign workers to companies looking for word processing or data entry professionals. What you haven't learned yet is easily picked up through a software tutorial provided at a temp agency workstation.

✯ Learn how to search on the Internet. As you prove your ability to handle basic tasks, you may be asked to help dig up additional information for an upcoming report or presentation.

✯ Pick up an office job, any office job. Even if it's just volunteer work with your local church, synagogue, mosque, or community center, get yourself into an office environment. Even if you're just filing papers or stuffing envelopes, an office environment will provide ample opportunity to get acquainted with office equipment—experience that will let you hit the ground running when you get your first word processing or data entry job.

What Training You'll Need

If you've made it through your English classes in high school, chances are you've already built some of the skills you'll need as a word processor. A solid grasp of spelling, grammar, and proper punctuation are critical for this career (Seek out current and classic references like the *Chicago Manual of Style, 15th Edition,* and *The Elements of Style,* and explore the many free grammar pages posted

The Inside Scoop: Q&A

Mark Regelski
Legal secretary/paralegal/word processor
New York City, New York

Q: *How did you get your job?*

A: Right after high school, I was employed by a temp agency. That's how a lot of this work happens and how you develop your skills. After starting at Blue Cross and Blue Shield, I was on call for word processing work because of my typing speed. By virtue of my ability to process words quickly, I got hired by a law firm. It started with a suggestion from an employment agency, really.

Q: *What do you like best about your job?*

A: Just the diversity of the work itself. It's an easy job to do, but it's difficult to do well. You get handed nothing but scribbled notes, and to turn it into a cohesive document is a real challenge; it's like doing a puzzle. What do I like about this job? As you get better at it, it's very easy to shine in this industry: If you're good at it, you're well above standard. For not having gone to college, the money is good, that's one of the benefits of working at a law firm. They treat you well. If you can turn things around quickly here, the lawyers just love you.

Q: *What's the most challenging part of your job?*

A: When it comes down to the work, it's not a glamorous function. It's not for everybody. Some people aren't cut out for office jobs, although it can be a challenge keeping abreast of all the technological changes in how documents are stored and treated. Being able to get along in a large group of different personalities can be a challenge. Every attorney thinks he or she is the most important person. If 300 attorneys are in the building, you have 300 people who think they're the most important person. The challenge is finding a great firm to work for, because really these jobs are a dime a dozen. The environments can be kind

(Continued on next page)

(continued from previous page)

of chaotic sometimes—what makes or breaks this kind of work is the people you work with.

Q: *What are the keys to success to being a word processor?*

A: In my opinion, you can't be a word processor who looks at the keyboard. What's made it easy for me is that my typing speed of over 100 words per minute has solved and defused any number of situations. Also, you have to be flexible and confident in working with people on all levels of authority or importance in a company. It can be very interesting sometimes while working on very important or confidential stuff, but you have to be able to function with people from the mailroom to the boardroom. Remember, when you're working with somebody, there's a customer service quality to it, and if they're happy, they'll be coming back the next day.

on the Web.) Because of the heavy amount of keyboard use in both of these jobs, check and see if your high school offers a course in typing. If you can work on getting your typing speed up to an impressive velocity while still achieving accuracy, you won't have to wait too long for your first job. If typing isn't a part of your school's curriculum or you've already graduated, don't worry. There are plenty of self-teaching CD-ROMs and books available at your local Barnes and Noble or Target for sharpening your typing or grammar skills. Most large companies and government agencies frequently have training programs to help word processors and data entry clerks upgrade their skills and upgrade their chances for advancing to higher-level positions.

How to Talk Like a Pro

Here are a few words you'll hear as a word processor or data entry clerk:

✯ **Embedded link** Also referred to as a hyperlink, an embedded link is a word processing device that allows objects (graphs, pictures) or words to be linked to another document or another section of the same document, or if the document is read online, the link can connect the reader to a page of a Web site.

- ✴ **Database** An organized and structured collection of records or data, which is stored in a computer so that a program can consult it to answer queries.
- ✴ **Spreadsheet** A grid for filling in and tracking information, typically financial data. Computer programs are now available that help users quickly calculate totals and perform other functions.

How to Find a Job

Almost 40 percent of professionals in this field either work for the state or local government or with a temporary agency. That's two out of every five jobs. A good place to start might be your local Yellow Pages. To get started in this field, you just need to call up a temp agency to make an appointment. Once you've been tested to evaluate your strengths, you'll receive a work assignment in an office environment ranging anywhere from a week to a few months. Many offices enlist the aid of temp agencies to help fill in during particularly busy times of the year, but they also use them as a way of getting to know the talents of a coworker before making a permanent hire. Beyond temp agencies, look into businesses that interest you. Every type of firm—from a record label to a film production company to a skateboard manufacturer—hires word processors. Legal services and elementary or secondary schools stand out as organizations that rely on word processors, according to the U.S. Department of Labor. If you would like to develop a specialty as a data entry clerk, opportunities are particularly high with insurance carriers, tax preparation firms, and accounting or bookkeeping firms.

Secrets for Success

See the following suggestions and turn to the appendix for advice on résumés and interviews.

- ✴ Be flexible. In the business world, priorities fluctuate constantly. What was once important one minute may be replaced by something even more important the next. As deadlines approach for presentations and reports, last-minute additions or subtractions are as plentiful as morning coffee. If you can be flexible and roll with sudden changes and pick up tasks as quick as you're asked to drop them, you'll go far in these careers.

✯ Keep up with the latest technology. In the information age computers and software change quickly. Study up on the newest systems and software.

Reality Check

Word processors and data entry clerks are effectively short-order data cooks who are expected to serve up documents to various specifications at a moment's notice. If you're uncomfortable with working on the fly and fielding a constant stream of requests, this job may not be for you.

Some Other Jobs to Think About

✯ Dispatcher. Dispatchers draw from the same skill set as word processors and data entry clerks by processing information quickly. Dispatchers schedule and—you guessed it—dispatch workers, equipment, or vehicles for the transport of passengers or goods. If you've ever ordered a taxi, you've spoken to a dispatcher.

✯ Court reporter. Court reporters perform tasks that are similar to word processors. Court reporters create word-for-word transcripts of legal proceedings, for which written accounts of speeches and conversations are needed for records, correspondence, or legal proofs.

How You Can Move Up

✯ Become a proofreader. After you've proven your commitment to detail and accuracy, look at becoming a proofreader. Government agencies and other publishers of documents need proofreaders as much as they need paper.

✯ Pursue a database administrator position. Once you've mastered the basics of entering, sorting, and processing information, you may be just a course or two away from becoming a database administrator. Building off your data entry expertise, you'll work with database management systems and determine the best ways to organize and store data.

Web Sites to Surf

International Association of Administrative Professionals. With a membership of 40,000 and counting, the association is a non-profit, professional networking and educational organization for office administration professionals. http://www.iaap-hq.org

National Association of Educational Office Professionals. This association has more than 40 offices across the country and provides learning and networking opportunities for office employees working in the field of education. http://www.naeop.org

Record monetary transactions

Account and Bill Collector

Handle vital company functions

Deal with a variety of people

Account and Bill Collector

Businesses cannot run if customers do not pay their bills, but frequently clients do not pay on time. That's where the account or bill collector steps in. As a collector, you help department stores, utility firms, hospitals, doctors, banks, and other organizations retrieve outstanding balances owed by customers. Either as an employee of a third-party collection agency or as direct employee of the original creditor, you'll locate and notify customers of delinquent accounts. When customers have a delinquent account, it means they owe money for a service or product and have not made payment by the agreed upon date. Collectors notify customers—usually with a phone call, or sometimes by drafting a letter. In extreme cases, collectors initiate repossession proceedings, discontinue the customer's service, or threaten legal action. It can be a difficult job, but ultimately you are there to help customers meet their financial obligations. Plus, the career provides a behind-the-scenes look at the financial world as you learn more about credit services. All you'll need for this occupation is an aptitude for interacting with the public and some basic computer skills. In this line of work, employers will provide you with the on-the-job training you need so you can begin in this new career right away.

Is This Job for You?

To find out if being an account or bill collector is a good fit for you, read each of the following questions and answer "Yes" or "No."

Yes	No	**1.**	Can you speak in a persuasive, polite, yet forceful tone?
Yes	No	**2.**	Are you comfortable interacting with strangers?
Yes	No	**3.**	Can you work unsupervised?
Yes	No	**4.**	Are you skilled with computers and software basics?
Yes	No	**5.**	If needed, do you think you could initiate repossession proceedings against a customer?
Yes	No	**6.**	Are you persistent?
Yes	No	**7.**	Do you have strong basic math skills?
Yes	No	**8.**	Do you think you would be good at educating others (specifically about the future implications of not paying bills)?

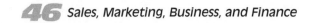

Let's Talk Money

According to 2006 data from the Bureau of Labor Statistics, collector wages average $13.20 per hour in the United States, adding up to an average annual salary of more than $27,400. The highest 10 percent earned around $33,800 per year. In addition to a base wage or salary, many collectors earn commissions determined on the amount of debt they recover.

Yes   No   **9.** Can you follow ethical guidelines as determined by the federal government?

Yes   No   **10.** Can you deal with rejection and/or talking with difficult customers?

If you answered "Yes" to most of these questions, consider a career as an account or bill collector. To find out more about these jobs, read on.

What You'll Do

As an account collector or billing adjustment clerk, you'll help keep track of overdue accounts and attempt to collect payment. You will likely work as either part of a collection agency or as an in-house representative of an organization. This could include working for a bank, hospital, physicians' office, retail store, government agency, or a utility like a gas, telephone, or electric company. Although your job will involve making phone calls to delinquent customers, your day will go far beyond that, because you have to find them first. Some customers will move without providing a forwarding address. Your job is to check with the post office, the telephone company, a credit bureau, or even former neighbors to try to locate where your customer currently resides. Once you've found your debtor, you work with the customer on a plan to make payments and overcome financial difficulties. Some credit card companies have a "hardship" payment program, in which they offer customers reduced rates for a limited period of time, provided the customer continues to success-fully make these lower payments. These payment programs are a key component in reestablishing a relationship with a customer.

They are a way of helping customers make good on a debt over a period of time. Collection agencies may also try to elicit payment by offering a discount on the bill if the customer can pay his or her bill in a lump sum.

Should you be successful in setting up a payment arrangement with the customer, it will be your job to record this commitment. You will need to keep track and verify that your customer made good on his or her promise to pay. If a customer is unwilling to make payment or unwilling to respond, collectors typically prepare statements indicating a customer's inaction. In extreme cases of delinquent accounts, collectors may begin proceedings to repossess property of the debtor or pass along the account to an attorney for legal action.

The work you do may be emotionally demanding. You'll be contacting people who owe money, so chances are you'll be speaking to people who are under a considerable amount of stress or who have recently suffered great hardship resulting from hospitalization, the loss of a job, or both. You'll need to walk the line between taking rejection well and taking into account a person's situation and seeing if you can find a payment arrangement that works for both sides.

Who You'll Work For

- ⭐ Banks
- ⭐ Retail stores
- ⭐ Physicians' offices
- ⭐ Hospitals
- ⭐ Collection agencies

Where You'll Work

Job environments depend largely on the type of employer you choose. If you work for a collection agency, chances are that you'll be

Let's Talk Trends

Collectors are in heavy demand, as companies ramp up their efforts to get moneys owed on unpaid accounts. According to the federal government, the field of 456,000 is expected to grow by 25 percent, adding more than 112,000 workers by 2014.

in a floor of cubicles surrounded by other callers. If you work as an in-house representative for an organization, you may be in a private office in a department store, bank, hospital, or auto insurance firm, for example.

If you are employed in a call center, the work atmosphere could be greatly affected by the shift you take. Evening is usually the busiest shift because customers are typically easier to contact during those hours. Collectors on the daytime shift may also have a heavy workload as they contact credit bureaus, post offices, and government agencies in an effort to locate customers. As a general rule though, most collection agencies and collection departments put in more hours during evenings and weekends when their success rate for reaching customers is generally higher.

Your Typical Day

Here are the highlights of a typical day at an office setting as either an account or bill collector.

✔ **Find your debtor.** Sometimes customers disappear without a trace or forwarding address. This means checking with the post office, utility company, credit bureaus, or even former neighbors to obtain new contact information.

✔ **Update records.** Once you've found your debtor, make sure your records are current.

✔ **Contact your customer and make a plan.** Often using a phone headset, you'll call your debtor and explain to him or her that their account is overdue. Once you've established contact, the next move is to take a payment and set up a plan to erase the debt over an extended period of time. If your customer is uncooperative, it will be your job to explain the potential consequences of their action and initiate repossession or legal proceedings.

✔ **Keep track of commitments.** Once you've gotten the debtor to agree to a plan of payments, you'll need to take notes of your conversation, which will be kept on file with the customer's account. This may also include recording the conversation or transferring the phone call to a supervisor who will sign-off on it and give the plan a final approval.

The Inside Scoop: Q&A

Debra J. Ciskey
Director of performance development group
Bloomington, Illinois

Q: *How did you get your job?*

A: I developed my specialized skills at another company and was recruited by the owner of my current company, who knew me as a result of the other work I [had done]. Most entry-level collectors get their jobs by replying to an ad in the paper or on the company Web site seeking collectors. Sometimes the positions are described as accounts receivable specialists or something similar.

Q: *What do you like best about your job?*

A: There is a lot of variety in the job of a collector. Collectors speak with 50 to 100 people each day on the telephone, and no two calls are alike. I love my job. I am responsible for developing the skills of supervisory and management staff, and I love to see them apply the new skills they learn in the classes I prepare for them.

Q: *What's the most challenging part of your job?*

A: We work with a lot of people who claim to be down and out— they have our bill and others in collections and don't know what to do. Our challenge is helping them think about and uncover resources they may not have realized are available to them so that they can pay their bills.

Q: *What are the keys to success to being an account collector?*

A: Successful collectors are persistent yet empathetic. They like working with all different kinds of people and they are creative thinkers and problem solvers. Collection professionals at the management level, just like managers in many small businesses, have to be willing to work hard. You must be very customer-oriented, and you must also be a good leader, because you are always being observed by your employees. You have to have a strong sense of integrity and fairness.

What You Can Do Now

★ If you're still in high school, consider taking a speech class. Part of your job will center on building an argument and speaking persuasively to help customers see your point of view.

★ Get yourself into an environment that will put your communication skills to the test. Employers in this field prefer candidates who have experience in jobs that involve contact with the general public. Working in customer service for a store is a good way to prepare.

★ Take a basic computer skills class. You can be the greatest speaker in the world, but if you don't have basic office computer skills, it won't matter. Step into your school's computer lab and start to get acquainted with the basics of Microsoft Office suite programs Word and Excel.

★ Take a typing class. Although your job will center on talking, you will need to take notes here and there to note progress on your accounts. If you are comfortable with your keyboard, it will keep you free to focus on other aspects of your job.

What Training You'll Need

In most instances, you'll need to have a high school diploma or equivalent to get a job as an account or bill collector. As a general rule, however, collection agencies or account departments of organizations like to hire workers who have at least some work experience that involves interacting with the public. After all, polished and persuasive communications skills will be the core of your job. Since this job requires frequent telephone usage, your ability to handle telecommunications fundamentals, such as transferring calls and teleconferencing, could demonstrate your level of seriousness in wanting to join their team.

Once you've received your "welcome aboard" handshake, you receive most of the tools you will need through a series of on-the-job training seminars. Typically under the guidance of a supervisor or experienced coworker, new employees are instructed on company procedures and any billing software. You need to master telephone techniques and ways of negotiating with customers. Collectors in training also learn the ins and outs of processing checks or credit card payments, locating people, and setting up payment plans.

How to Talk Like a Pro

Here are a few words you'll hear as an account or bill collector:

- ⚡ **Skip-tracing** If you're attempting to track down the current address of a delinquent customer who has vanished without a trace, this is a practice referred to in the trade as "skip-tracing." These days, new computer systems assist in tracing people by tracking when customers change their address or contact information on any of their open accounts.
- ⚡ **Fair Debt Collection Practices Act** Established in 1978, the Fair Debt Collection Practices Act is part of the Consumer Credit Protection Act. The act creates guidelines under which debt collectors may conduct business.
- ⚡ **In-house/third-party collector** In-house collectors work directly for the original creditors, such as department stores, hospitals, or banks. Third-party collectors typically work in a call center on behalf of another institution.

How to Find a Job

When looking into the rapidly expanding career field of account and bill collecting, you should survey where the need for collectors is growing the fastest. As insurance reimbursements fail to keep up with cost increases, hospitals and physicians' offices are two of the fastest-growing areas in need of collection help as the health care industry seeks to recover more money from patients. Not wanting to be left out, government agencies are also enlisting collection professionals to collect on everything ranging from outstanding parking tickets to overdue child-support payments and back taxes. If you have a particular interest in learning more about the health care industry or government agencies, you may want to get on the Internet and start looking for the homepages of your local hospital, clinic, or government agencies.

If you feel like your computer skills could use a bit more work or if you've been told that you need a reference from an employer, you may want to consider joining a temporary staffing agency. After proving yourself as a responsible worker you will be a more attractive hire to the collection agencies and departments in your area. Also, you may

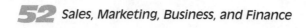

want to contact the Association of Credit and Collection Professionals and see if they have any career advice to offer. We've listed the Web site at the end of this chapter. Internet search engines and job sites such as Monster.com or craigslist.org are potentially useful sources to check as well.

Secrets for Success

See the following suggestions and turn to the appendix for advice on résumés and interviews.

⭑ Show some understanding. A little empathy can go a long way in this career. As you make your calls, keep in mind that many of the people you'll be contacting may be hip deep in debt as a result of losing their job or some other problem. Keep in mind that a call from a collection agency or debt collector is hardly a pleasant thought for many. You'll get a lot further in your efforts to collect payment and/or set up a payment plan if you can present yourself in a pleasant manner and as someone who is on their side and trying to help rebuild their credit rating.

⭑ Track agreements carefully. When you do reach a payment plan with a debtor, carefully record the new terms and make sure the customer sticks to them.

Reality Check

If you're not prepared for the potential stress of a heated discussion, you may want to look at one of our other career chapters. Although you will talk to people who are willing to work with you, some customers can be confrontational when pressed into discussing their debts.

Some Other Jobs to Think About

⭑ Credit authorizer/credit checker. These professionals obtain the information needed to determine the creditworthiness of individuals or businesses applying for credit.

⭑ Customer service representative. In this career, you are helping people solve problems with a product or service.

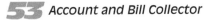

How You Can Move Up

* Become a supervisor. Most collection agencies or departments rarely go outside to fill supervisory positions. Instead, they prefer to promote those who already know the system and have an established track record of debt-collecting success.
* Step up as a collection agency manager. Once you've strutted your stuff as a supervisor and demonstrated a broad understanding of how the collection industry works, consider throwing your hat into the management ring.

Web Sites to Surf

The Association of Credit and Collection Professionals. Founded in 1939, the Association of Credit and Collection Professionals draws from its stable of third-party collection agencies, asset buyers, and creditors to provide training and set ethical standards in the credit and collection industry. The site also provides a host of Web courses, training products, and online seminars. http://www.acainternational.org

Creditboards.com. This Web site provides a forum for discussion on the latest issues in credit and debt collection, providing newsfeeds and a selection of archived articles on the topics of credit and debt collection. http://www.creditboards.com

Work with money

Retail Associate/Cashier

Greet people on a daily basis

Learn the basics of sales

Retail Associate/Cashier

Cashiers are really the backbone of the consumer world. Retailers rely on sales associates to handle the transactions on which their businesses depend. Without good cashiers, chain stores like the Gap, Radio Shack, Rite Aid, Costco, and local grocery stores and gas stations could not survive. With a good head for math, these professionals take care of cash and credit card purchases at the register, and they help customers make buying decisions. By providing shoppers with information on products, paying attention to their needs, and simply being friendly, associates can often increase sales. Some will even earn a commission on top of salary for the sales they make. When it comes to employment opportunities, this occupation is one of the largest, with a combined 7.8 million jobs and new positions opening up daily, according to the U.S. Bureau of Labor Statistics, businesses in almost every city and town hire cashiers. Regardless of the employer, as a retail associate, you can learn the ins and outs of a business while playing an important role in providing specialized customer service and ensuring customer satisfaction. Although turnover can be quite high in this profession, those who stick to the job and perform their duties well can advance from trainee to manager in no time.

Is This Job for You?

To find out if being a retail associate or cashier is a good fit for you, read each of the following questions and answer "Yes" or "No."

Yes	No	**1.**	Do you enjoy helping people find what they want?
Yes	No	**2.**	Can you take direction from others?
Yes	No	**3.**	Can you be patient with a line of customers?
Yes	No	**4.**	Are you capable of constant light lifting (possibly shelving products)?
Yes	No	**5.**	Do you enjoy meeting people from many different backgrounds?
Yes	No	**6.**	Are you comfortable with handling money?
Yes	No	**7.**	Are you dependable and organized?
Yes	No	**8.**	Are you flexible and willing to work nights and weekends?

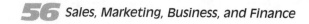

Let's Talk Money

Retail associate wages average around $8 an hour, with cashiers usually starting around minimum wage (which is $5.15, although 18 states have passed laws which require a higher minimum wage). According to 2006 data from the Bureau of Labor Statistics, cashiers earn about $16,000 a year, with department store workers and building supply store workers earning a little bit more with annual incomes of $17,500 and $22,500, respectively. Full-time cashiers and retail associates usually receive health care benefits; part-time workers traditionally do not.

Yes   No   **9.** Would you enjoy helping other coworkers as needed?

Yes   No   **10.** Are you good at doing simple math in your head (assuring that you can provide the correct change)?

If you answered "Yes" to most of these questions, consider a career as a retail associate/cashier. To find out more about this job, read on.

What You'll Do

In a retail store, associates and cashiers are the first contact point for most customers. They greet shoppers, answer questions in the aisles, and take payments at the register, while also handling customer returns and exchanges.

Basic math skills and good communications are essential at this job as you meet a wide variety of new people on a daily basis and handle a stream of purchases. Running a cash register and processing credit card transactions requires attention to detail. Often you do the same type of task over and over again. Depending on the nature of the business, cashiers and retail associates may get moved throughout the store during the day. Workers may be asked to return abandoned items to shelves or to assist in building a display for a product that's on sale. Positions at convenience stores and service stations may demand more multitasking, from issuing money orders to selling lottery tickets.

Although in a retail setting, you will most certainly be assigned to a register for a good portion of your day, you may be asked to restock shelves, conduct product inventory, or help out with general house-keeping chores such as emptying wastebaskets and the like.

Who You'll Work For

* Department stores
* Supermarkets
* Movie theatres
* Restaurants
* Gas stations
* Convenience stores

Where You'll Work

Ka-ching! That's the sound of a cash register and it's music to the ears of your store manager. You could be sitting behind a window at a movie theatre box office selling tickets, or you could be ringing up blue jeans, school supplies, or cat toys. Although many cashiers work in department and retail stores, 27 percent of all jobs were in food and beverage stores, according to the Bureau of Labor Statistics. Beyond retail stores, cashiers labor in government office (like the Department of Motor Vehicles), amusement parks, casinos, and recreation services. Although 9-to-5 shifts are available, peak hours are typically evenings and weekends, so if you're just starting out, those may be the times you're asked to work.

Let's Talk Trends

The need for retail associates and cashiers is expected to grow at a rate of 9 to 17 percent until 2014, according to the Bureau of Labor Statistics. Although many customers do their shopping on the Internet, computers cannot replace the need for customer service and associate expertise. Opportunities for full-time and part-time cashier jobs should continue to be strong in an industry where many openings are created by those seeking out work as a short-term or seasonal source of income.

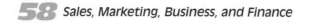

Your Typical Day

Here are the highlights for a typical day for a cashier or retail associate.

✔ **Set up your drawer.** At the beginning of a shift, cashiers are usually assigned to a register and given drawers containing a specific allotment of money with which to start. If you're running low on ones and fives, give your assistant manager or store manager a shout—it's hard to make change for customers when you only have ten- and twenty-dollar bills.

✔ **Handle customer service/returns and exchanges.** Provide an ear for customers as they bring an issue of concern to your attention and explain why they are returning an item. You will be responsible for learning your store's return policy and will use your judgment as to whether customers have valid reasons for returning items.

✔ **Stock shelves.** You may have to lend a hand putting merchandise on display.

✔ **Answer questions.** Customers often have questions about products. You need to be familiar with products that the store sells so you can respond to shoppers' inquiries.

✔ **Act as a trend-spotter.** Impress your boss by keeping an eye out for consumer behavior. If during the summer months you notice your store is almost always out of bottled water after every weekend, then pipe up and tell your manager that more needs to be ordered. Even if your manager has noticed this too, she or he will be happy to know they have an employee who is really paying attention.

What You Can Do Now

✴ Brush up on your math skills. Focus on examples involving the exchange of money.

✴ Place yourself in settings where you will be exposed to people of diverse ages and backgrounds.

✴ If there's a store or industry that interests you, learn more about them by doing some research on the Internet.

✴ Get a part-time job in a convenience store, department store, clothes shop, or any other retail environment.

The Inside Scoop: Q&A

Marv Hutchens
Assistant store manager
Brooklyn Park, Minnesota

Q: *How did you get your job?*

A: I had worked in retail and held customer service jobs previously, so they liked the experience I'd had with the buying public. I was looking for a little extra income, and they were looking for an overnight manager. They said, "We need somebody like you," and they hired me. I happened to be in the right place at the right time.

Q: *What do you like best about your job?*

A: I do all the end-of-day money and bank deposits. Handling the money and balancing the books is a big responsibility, and I like that.

Q: *What's the most challenging part of your job?*

A: Although balancing the books can be a challenge sometimes, handling a customer situation where they're upset about something is hard. I don't get a lot of that, but that's probably the most challenging. You have to make sure to make the customer happy, but you've got to watch out for the store's best interest as well.

Q: *What are the keys to success for being a retail associate and cashier?*

A: I think you have to be detail-oriented and organized. I guess you have to be willing to take on whatever task needs to be done. There's a wide variety of stuff that I do. Particularly if you work overnight, you have to be somewhat self-motivated. Normally, the people higher than you in management aren't going to be there supervising you.

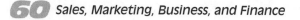

What Training You'll Need

Cashier and retail associate jobs are typically the starting or entry-level position at a store or establishment, requiring very little or even no work experience. The need for cashiers or counter help can often be quite high. As with some other careers (including telemarketing, which is covered in Chapter 7), employers are desperate to find new talent and are often willing to provide the training you'll need. As the turnover can be quite high, those who show promise and invest the time to learn about the job and the workings of the store can advance to positions of greater responsibility. As a new member of the store team, it's likely you'll spend your first days as an observer, taking notes on how things operate while becoming familiar with the store's equipment and policies. Length and depth of training can vary depending on the size of your establishment. Larger chains frequently require their trainees to attend classes before being assigned a cash register. If that's the case, you can expect an overview of the industry and discussion of store rules, equipment, and—last but not least—security. In addition to learning to operate the register, cashiers typically will be trained on how to process coupons and discounts or how to sign customers up for credit cards. They may also learn how to process payments with credit cards, debit cards, and personal checks. If employed by convenience stores, gas stations, and supermarkets cashiers are likely to be trained on how to deal with age verification for customers purchasing alcohol or tobacco.

How to Talk Like a Pro

Here are a few words to know as a retail associate or cashier:

* **Till** The drawer of money assigned to a register at the beginning of a shift. Tills require counting to make sure they have the correct amount of cash and enough change for customer purchases.
* **Z-report** The sum total cash register report for the shift or day. It's usually accomplished by the key holder (usually an assistant or store manager) inserting their key into a lock on the register and turning it to the letter Z, which then instructs the register to add up all conducted financial activity.
* **Cash drop/Pick-up** When your register is overflowing with too many big bills, it's time to call your manager over for a "pick-up." He or

she then puts a closed sign at your register and conducts a re-port and places the excess money into an envelope, which is then brought to a safe. A manager produces a receipt that records the details of all "pick-ups."

How to Find a Job

So many retail opportunities are available that you can often get an entry-level job in a store selling the type of products that interest you—food, CDs, clothes, shoes, furniture, bikes, skateboards, or other things. If there's some place you'd really like to work, it never hurts to put on some of your best clothes, ask to speak to the store manager, and inquire if they're hiring. Presentation is a large part of sales and if they're impressed with how you carry yourself, they'll take notice even if they're not hiring at the moment. Good retail man-agers are always keeping an eye out for new talent. If a store you'd like to work at isn't hiring, ask if you can fill out an application to place on file should a position become available.

If there's a particular store or industry you want to be a part of, get on the Internet and do a little research before heading in to make that ever-important first impression. Also, look for opportunities listed on Internet job sites, such as Monster.com. Don't forget your local newspaper's classified section—it's worth a look and the online version may be searchable by category or key word. (These days, many jobs can be applied for online.) If you want to test the waters as a cashier, you might first look into a temporary or part-time position.

Secrets for Success

See the following suggestions and turn to the appendix for advice on résumés and interviews.

☆ Show some simple kindness. It may sound cliché, but if you treat customers like you want to be treated, that behavior can increase sales. Be understanding, patient, and accommodating to the wide variety of customer needs. You will impress those around you (including your manager), and make a strong case for being trusted with greater responsibility and opportunity.

☆ Be prompt. It may be a simple thing but being on time really im-presses people and shows that you are responsible.

Reality Check

Retail associates and cashiers are needed most when the traditional 9-to-5 world gets off work. If you want weekends and evenings off, this probably isn't the field for you. The more flexible you can be in your scheduling to pick up shifts, the greater the value you'll have for your store, increasing your challenges for taking on more responsibility and possibly a bigger paycheck in the future. Plus, are you good at figuring out what change you should get back when you go shopping? It pays to be quick with simple addition and subtraction to excel as a cashier.

Some other Jobs to Think About

* Hotel and resort worker. Workers in this field register arriving guests, assign rooms, and check out guests at the end of their stay. Record-keeping is involved, which is a more computer-oriented system of cashier work and customer service. Typically, handling telephones and fielding questions from tourists or convention visitors is part of the job as well.

* Grocery store stock clerk. Grocery store workers stock shelves with merchandise and build product displays to attract customers. Workers assist customers in locating or demonstrating various items.

* Receptionist and information clerk. These are the people who make the first impression that a visitor to an organization or business encounters. The position often includes answering telephones, routing calls, light typing or clerical work, greeting visitors, and providing information to the general public.

How You Can Move Up

* Become a head cashier. In this position, you oversee other cashiers, and you'll be responsible for ordering change, preparing bank deposits, processing charge card receipts, and ensuring that registers have adequate cash for operations.

* Seek an assistant manager position. Many retail chains have training programs designed to promote you to this position. This job can translate into more responsibility, more money, and the opportunity to become a store manager within the organization.

✯ Apply to be a store manager. Store managers know the ins and outs of the store, and are responsible for its daily operation, ordering goods, monitoring inventory, and making staffing decisions. Typically store managers are given a percentage incentive to share in a store's financial success.

Web Sites to Surf

Retail Worker/Labor News A project of the Industrial Workers of the World labor union, this site acts as a resource and online community, providing opportunities to connect with others in your field. The site provides bulletin boards for posting questions on topics, including hourly wages for various positions. http://www.retailworker.com

Monster.com A national job Web site offering a keyword search engine for listing jobs posted by retailers. By using a keyword search, potential employees can target openings in fields that most interest them. http://www.monster.com

Talk with a variety of people

Telemarketer

Develop excellent sales skills

Build oral communication skills

Telemarketer

Businesses of all types and sizes are always looking for ways to per-suade customers to purchase a particular good or service. Telemar-keting—or selling by phone—has proven to be one of the most effective means for boosting sales, although we all know those calls at the dinner hour can be annoying at times. Through the power of com-munications and traditional sales techniques, telemarketers engage potential customers in a dialogue with the goal of convincing the con-sumer to try a product or service—whether it be a magazine sub-scription, cell phone service, aluminum siding, car insurance, or a new brand of coffee. They ply their skill not only with businesses but also with charities, political campaigns, media organizations, and even the local museums and orchestras who are looking to expand membership. Today, about 400,000 telemarketers work keeping the phone lines buzzing with their pitches, and new positions are grow-ing, according to 2006 data from the U.S. Bureau of Labor Statistics. The job usually involves a lot of rejection, but professionals enjoy both talking with a variety of people and the thrill of clinching a sale. If you're confident, self-motivated, and love talking to strangers, tele-marketing may be a perfect career match, and the training you'll need is usually provided by your employer. With a few days of on-the-job lessons, you can grab your phone headset and step into this new job right away.

Is This Job for You?

To find out if being a telemarketer is a good fit for you, read each of the following questions and answer "Yes" or "No."

Yes	*No*	**1.**	Do you enjoy talking to new people?
Yes	*No*	**2.**	Are you comfortable with introducing yourself to strangers?
Yes	*No*	**3.**	Can you manage your time effectively?
Yes	*No*	**4.**	Are you comfortable with computers and software basics, such as the Microsoft Office suite programs Word and Excel?
Yes	*No*	**5.**	Can you handle rejection and move on to the next call?
Yes	*No*	**6.**	Are you self-motivated?

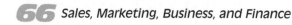

Let's Talk Money

According to 2006 data from the Bureau of Labor Statistics, telemarketers earned $13.18 an hour, or $24,966 per year. The top 10 percent earned more than $37,500 per year. As sales targets are met, telemarketers receive bonuses and sales commissions. Some employers offer a 401(k) plan.

Yes	*No*	**7.**	Are you willing to learn sales techniques?
Yes	*No*	**8.**	Can you be productive under minimal supervision?
Yes	*No*	**9.**	Are you good at persuading people to see a point of view?
Yes	*No*	**10.**	Can you work in a fast-paced environment?

If you answered "Yes" to most of these questions, consider a career as a telemarketer. To find out more about this job, read on.

What You'll Do

As a telemarketer, you sell anything over the phone from newspaper subscriptions to opera season tickets to air conditioners. With a headset that's most likely connected to a computer, you call your way through a list of prospective customers. Sometimes, the computer is programmed to dial numbers for you to save you time and energy. After introducing yourself as a company representative, you direct the conversation to discussing the customer's needs and suggest how your company's services or merchandise can help fulfill them. "Are you not getting enough local news coverage?" "Would you like our cable package so you don't miss out on the big game this Friday?" "How much is your current auto insurance company charging, because we could save you money?" These are just a few examples of questions you might ask as a telemarketer.

Not all telemarketing calls involve making a direct sale to the customer. Instead your call may be geared toward arranging an appointment between the prospective client and outside sales representative. This is common in the sale of large household appliances or security systems. However, not all telemarketers engage strictly in sales. A great many of them work in the field of market research. Your agency

may provide you with a list of numbers from customers who have made major purchases. For example, you may end up calling someone to inquire if they're still happy with their recent purchase of a refrigerator or dishwasher. From a screen of numbered responses, you'll select the customer's level of satisfaction, and if they're unhappy you'll need to take notes that will be entered into the system and sent to your supervisor.

Presentation and persuasion are the crucial aspects of this career. Simply conveying warmth, concern, and friendliness can help you connect with a customer. Telemarketing is, in effect, a training ground for future sales professionals. Part-time positions are almost always available in this field. If you're unsure if this field is a good fit, look at establishing a plan of working 20 hours per week or try out the morning, afternoon, or evening shifts to see what will work best for you.

Who You'll Work For

* Electronic shopping and mail-order centers
* Telephone call centers
* Business service centers
* Security/home alarm agencies
* Mortgage companies
* Political campaigns
* Charitable organizations
* Alumni associations
* Marketing research companies
* Newspapers, cable companies

Let's Talk Trends

Telemarketers are always in big demand. With more than 4,700 telemarketing organizations employing 400,000 telemarketing professionals nationwide, new positions are multiplying. Although more telemarketing is being outsourced to operations overseas, opportunities in marketing are expected to grow faster than the average for all occupations through 2014, according to 2006 Bureau of Labor Statistics data.

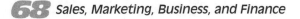

Where You'll Work

The vast majority of jobs in this field are at call centers equipped with workstation cubicles. Cubicles often come decorated with sheets of fluorescent paper outlining call or sales procedures to help employees develop their customer approach with a minimal amount of hesitation. The more you learn the routine by heart, the more persuasive you'll be and the quicker you'll make your sales quotas.

A great many of these environments operate 24–7, and the shift you take could also play a major role in your environment. Day shifts can be a bit slow, with a fair amount of interaction with either the self-employed or homemakers, who may or may not be your target audience. Late afternoon shifts, from 4 p.m. to 12 a.m., are typically a busier period as people start to arrive home from work. Some telemarketers work as a branch of a company, such as a subscription service for a newspaper. As business starts to pick up, your work environment could become quite noisy as calls start to reach the target audience with greater frequency. For the most part, you will work under minimal supervision, interacting with supervisors from time to time to either help close a sale or answer a customer inquiry. From time to time, supervisors will listen in on your calls to evaluate your performance.

Take note that some telemarketing firms are dedicated to making cold calls. Cold calls are the most challenging to make because you must contact customers with whom the company has no previous relationship. Other organizations will have you contact only already established accounts, and some may have you call a mix of both.

Because your job is almost entirely dependent upon a computer and a telephone, it's entirely possible that you can work from home, provided you continue to satisfy your employer's sales quotas.

Your Typical Day

Here are the highlights of a typical day at an office setting as a telemarketer.

- ✔ **Get your call list.** You have to have your list of numbers to call ready to go.
- ✔ **Make those appointments.** This is particularly true if you are doing telemarketing work for a company selling goods that require

The Inside Scoop: Q & A

Tim Searcy
Telemarketing company principal
Indianapolis, Indiana

Q: *How did you get your job?*

A: I grew up in Omaha, Nebraska, which is (or was) the teleservices capital of the world. My newspaper route needed some beefing up, so my route manager encouraged me to join some other guys on the phones at the newspaper offices to drum up some business. My first commission was a 164-piece, multicolor marker set. I was 10 at the time. I was able to take inbound calls for products like Ginsu knives and bamboo steamers when I was 14, and by the time I was 16, I was working for Dial America Marketing selling magazines.

Q: *What do you like best about your job?*

A: Unless you are a professional athlete, very few jobs can give you the immediate feedback that telemarketing can. This is a business that keeps track of everything related to performance and highly trains and motivates its personnel to get better. Telemarketing is the fastest-growing branch of the fastest growing sector (the services industry) in the United States. The role is highly efficient for someone interested in career advancement. Teleservices only cares about performance and attitude, which lets anyone succeed.

Q: *What's the most challenging part of your job?*

A: Rejection is difficult. However, the challenge is also the reward because when you can solve a customer's problem or turn around their negative attitude about a company, or sell them a competitive product at a better price, it all seems worth it.

Q: *What are the keys to success to being a telemarketer?*

A: Teleservices is a straightforward business and needs to be treated as such by the professional interested in making a career in this business. If an individual will follow the training, take coaching on the job, show up on time, keep score like the boss does

(Continued on next page)

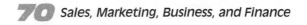

(continued from previous page)

concerning performance, and exhibit a positive attitude, the sky is the limit. The industry continues to aggressively seek the person wanting to make a career, and a modicum of enthusiasm will be rewarded with a maximum response from an employer.

in-home demonstrations. After you've successfully established a connection with a customer interested in what you're offering, it'll be your job to coordinate your potential customer's schedule with your in-home sales staff.

✔ **Generate those leads.** The first call is usually the most important, when you will help determine a customer's need. Customers interested in product demonstrations or who express interest but who have not yet paid are referred to as "leads." Leads are hot property in the telemarketing profession and pave the way to making an effective second call to close the sale.

✔ **Try, try, and try again.** Some prospective customers you're trying to reach may need several calls before you finally get a hold of them. Much of your day will center on contacting customers to discuss their needs and their potential interest in what you're selling. Or your calls could center on a customer's level of satisfaction with a good or service recently purchased.

What You Can Do Now

✶ Take a typing class that will improve your speed and accuracy skills. Typing comes in handy if you need to take notes on your conversation with a customer.

✶ Complete an accounting class. This will improve your ability for processing payments.

✶ Get a job in a retail setting. This will provide you with opportunities to develop your sales skills by interacting with customers and explaining a line of products or services.

✶ Look for a part-time or summer job in telemarketing. Test the waters and see if phone work is for you. You might want to volunteer for a cause that interests you—environmental groups, political organizations, medical research teams, and other nonprofits all use telemarketers to seek donations and raise awareness.

What Training You'll Need

Although it wouldn't hurt to have sales background to start, most call centers or other firms employing telemarketers are simply looking for good communications and presentation skills. If you can demonstrate a good attitude and showcase strong presentation and persuasion skills, your employer will be happy to provide you with the tools you need so you can hit the ground running. It's as simple as reading off a computer screen and making a phone call. You just need to be able to type a little bit and you'll be set.

How to Talk Like a Pro

Here are a few words you'll hear as a telemarketer:

* **Call centers** Organizations that only make phone calls on the behalf of other companies for a fee.
* **Inbound/outbound** These are the two types of calls made in telemarketing. Inbound calls focus on receiving incoming orders and requests for information. Outbound calls involve contacting prospective and preexisting customers directly.
* **Lead generation** If your phone call collects information that leads to a potential sale or product demonstration, you are engaging in a practice known as "lead generation."
* **National Do Not Call Registry** Passed as law in 2003, the National Do Not Call Registry requires most telemarketers to remove telephone numbers on the registry from their call lists. However, telemarketers may still contact persons on the "Do Not Call" list provided they are either a telephone surveyor, or if they are calling on behalf of a political organization, charity, or a business with which the person has an existing business relationship.

How to Find a Job

Finding telemarketing work may be less obvious than finding a retail or bank teller job, but not to worry. First, ask yourself if there's a particular field to which you'd like to lend your talents. Do you want to help raise money for the local symphony or museum? Or is there a charity for which you'd like to help raise funds? Perhaps you'd rather take a shot at learning more about your local newspaper? If you can target an organization that interests you, just type its name into

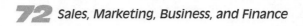

Google or Yahoo! and start looking through their homepage and search for a link to the "jobs" page. If you don't have a specific organization or type of telemarketing job in mind, you can either consult the jobs section of your local newspaper or use an Internet job search engine such as Monster.com, CareerBuilder.com, or even the online classifieds of your local newspaper. Just type in the word telemarketer, telemarketing, or call center, and you'll be flooded with results. Many of these job pages accept applications online. Also, many temporary work agencies staff telemarketing call centers, and these centers are frequently hiring.

Secrets for Success

See the following suggestions and turn to the appendix for advice on résumés and interviews.

- ✴ Take frequent, but short breaks. Sitting down and reading off a computer screen for a lengthy period of time offers potential for back, neck, and wrist aches. Most call centers know this and allow their employees an opportunity to unplug for a few minutes each hour. Be sure to make the most of your breaks and go for a walk. If your eyes, neck, and back aren't complaining, you'll be in a far better position to be a persuasive telemarketer.
- ✴ Maintain your voice. Drink fluids throughout the day and give yourself some rest periods. Your voice is your most valuable tool in this job so you will want to keep it in proper working order.

Reality Check

Can you handle the sting of rejection? Repeatedly? Good. In this job, you will talk with people who are interested in hearing what you have to say, while others may be quite rude in communicating with you. The important thing is to not take rejection or rudeness personally and keep moving ahead to the next potential sale.

Some Other Jobs to Think About

- ✴ Receptionist. In addition to clerical work and greeting visitors, these professionals field calls and handle customer inquiries.
- ✴ Reservation and transportation ticket agents. Reservation and transportation ticket agents work in large reservation centers for

hotel chains or airlines. These agents field incoming calls and assess customer needs. These agents offer suggestions on types of accommodation, quoting fares and room rates while providing travel information such as routes, schedules, and rates.

- ✴ Travel agent. Travel agents perform tasks that are similar to telemarketers. This field relies heavily on sales professionals to field incoming calls and help customers assess their needs and help plan their travel arrangements.

How You Can Move Up

- ✴ Become a call center trainer. After you've demonstrated your mastery of sales techniques, consider working as a coach or teacher by providing the training needed to help employees reach their sales goals.
- ✴ Seek a promotions manager position. Once you've learned to entice customers and built a record of meeting sales quotas, you may be able to help establish closer contact with dealers, distributors, and consumers of goods by designing a promotions program centered on telemarketing and direct mail.

Web Sites to Surf

American Teleservices Association. Complete with a classified section and a career center, the association's Web site provides a list of local membership chapters that support professionals in telemarketing and other phone-related industries. They even offer podcasts to keep professionals up-to-date on this always-evolving industry. http://www.ataconnect.org

Direct Marketing Association. This global trade organization of business and nonprofit organizations details all the latest issues involving direct marketing tools, including telemarketing. The site also includes a handy page of links providing information about do-not-call laws in each state. http://www.the-dma.org

Deal with the public

Customer Service Representative

Represent a retailer or other business

Understand corporate policy

Customer Service Representative

Customer service representatives are at the core of an organization's reputation. Every satisfied and repeat customer starts with good customer service. Whether by telephone, at a desk, or out on the sales floor, these representatives establish a vital connection between customer and company. Professionals in this field listen carefully to shoppers and try to see how they can best meet their concerns, complaints, and needs. At the same time, they work within a firm's guidelines and do what they can to advance their employer's business. They must be very familiar with the products and services offered by their employers. Because much of the world's shopping activity takes place after normal 9-to-5 business hours, nearly one out of five professionals in this field work part-time and the career frequently includes evenings, weekends, and holidays. As a result, employers frequently offer flexible work schedules. Today, about 2.1 million customer service reps work in the United States, and new positions are on the rise, according to 2006 data from the U.S. Bureau of Labor Statistics. If you have the right talents, you can step into a customer service job with just a high school diploma. Primarily, you need to be friendly and courteous, a good listener, and familiar with your firm's products and policies.

Is This Job for You?

To find out if being a customer service representative is a good fit for you, read each of the following questions and answer "Yes" or "No."

Yes *No* **1.** Do you enjoy working in a busy and potentially noisy environment?

Yes *No* **2.** Are you interested in learning how a business works?

Yes *No* **3.** Are you willing to work evenings, weekends, and holidays?

Yes *No* **4.** Are you comfortable with computers and software basics, such as Microsoft Office suite programs Word and Excel?

Yes *No* **5.** Can you perform repetitive tasks with great accuracy?

Yes *No* **6.** Can you listen to person's complaints without taking them personally?

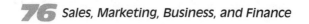

Let's Talk Money

Wages for customer service representatives vary as much as the industries for which they work. The insurance field typically pays 25 percent more to their specialized staff. Wages in this field averaged $12.98 an hour in the United States, according to 2006 data from the Bureau of Labor Statistics. Reps earn an average of about $27,020 per year, with the highest 10 percent earning more than $44,100 per year. Those who work evenings, nights, weekends, or holidays may receive slightly higher wages. Benefits can include insurance, pensions, and employee discounts.

Yes   No   **7.** Are you well organized and able to keep track of records?

Yes   No   **8.** Does seeing another person's point of view come easily?

Yes   No   **9.** Would you enjoy a job where you talk for most of the day?

Yes   No   **10.** Are you good at finding solutions and dealing with people who may be difficult?

If you answered "Yes" to most of these questions, consider a career as a customer service representative. To find out more about this job, read on.

What You'll Do

As a customer service rep, you must be a library of information to field all questions and concerns. You serve as a direct point of contact between the customer and your employer. A customer's willingness to become a repeat customer or recommend your company's products or services to others may depend entirely on your quality of customer care. Just as businesses vary in what they offer, so do the roles of these reps. Some are hooked-up to telephones and headsets in customer call centers; others provide support at a help desk or kiosk at a megastore or shopping mall. In retail settings such as Brookstone, Home Depot, or Best Buy, customer service pros may provide a more hands-on approach as they demonstrate how a product works or why one product may be better than another in meeting a shopper's needs.

When a customer is angry, frustrated, or just determined to be difficult, your job is to lend an ear and look for an opportunity to help resolve the situation. Your underlying purpose is to keep customers happy and coming back for more. If they're not satisfied, it'll be your job to find out why and propose a way within company guidelines to make the customer feel understood and valued. Most companies have procedures in place for resolving problems. You may consult a list of questions that will help evaluate the validity of a complaint. You may need to study guidelines that explain when it is appropriate to provide refunds, discounts, or exchanges.

The work you do may be physically and emotionally draining, as some shoppers can be difficult and demanding. Representatives should be comfortable with doing two things at once: If you work at a call center, you'll need to be able to talk while taking notes or searching for information on your customer. If you work in a more traditional retail setting, it's possible that you could field questions via telephone while helping to ring up sales at the counter.

Who You'll Work For

- Financial services
- Insurance carriers
- Insurance agencies
- Banks
- Credit unions
- General merchandise stores
- Telecommunications operations
- Temporary agencies
- Call centers

Let's Talk Trends

Because there are more openings than prospective employees in this profession, customer service reps are in huge demand, and the opportunities are even greater if you speak a second language. Fluency in Spanish can be especially attractive as the Latino market is booming. By 2014, expect to see more than 546,000 new positions, according to 2006 Bureau of Labor Statistics data.

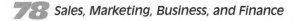

Where You'll Work

Customer service reps are most visible at department stores, supermarkets, and other retailers, such as CD shops and clothing outlets. These reps walk the floors of air-conditioned venues, ready to answer questions and take care of shoppers' problems. They deal with a continuous flow of various customers. They spend time off the sales floor meeting with coworkers to discuss store policies, latest sales efforts, and any recurring problems that customers may have voiced.

A high percentage of workers in this field have their own workstation in a customer contact center, equipped with a computer, telephone, and a headset. Call centers never sleep—most typically stay open beyond the traditional workday. Many of them buzz with activity around the clock, such as some banks or insurance companies. As a result, your job environment could be affected greatly by the early morning, evening, or late-night shift you take. Good sitters excel at this job—the work requires long periods in front of a computer monitor, typing up notes on the conversations you have with customers.

Although reps can be found pretty much anywhere products and services are provided, it should be noted that a particularly high concentration of call centers are in California, Florida, Texas, and New York. Also, according to the U.S. Department of Labor, customer service positions for one out of every 50 jobs in the states of Delaware, Arizona, South Dakota, and Utah.

Your Typical Day

Here are the highlights of a typical day as a customer service representative:

✔ **They've got questions, you've got answers.** If you hear the phone ringing, there's a good chance it's for you. If you work in a retail setting, such as a hardware store, it'll be your job to answer inquiries about merchandise or services. In many instances, it'll be your responsibility to evaluate a customer's question and direct the call to the proper department.

✔ **They've still got questions and you need answers.** When fielding questions either by phone or in person, you may come across a topic that's beyond what you're able to handle. This occurs typically when a billing or exchange question is involved. Learning when to ask for help and bring in a supervisor is a crucial part of your job.

The Inside Scoop: Q & A

Chantel Scheen
Service delivery coordinator
Seattle, Washington

Q: *How did you get your job?*

A: I like talking to people. I figured, "Hey, I can talk on the phone," so I started out as a hotel operator. I went to a hotel in downtown Seattle and visited their human resources department. Then, while working in a hospital as an operator, I saw there was an opening at Qwest, so I applied and here I am.

Q: *What do you like best about your job?*

A: I enjoy working with people. I like finding the answers and talking with customers on the phone or through e-mail, even if it's an issue a person is upset about. Helping a customer figure out what's going on is always fun. You get to know them a bit better and through knowing people it expands your worldview.

Q: *What's the most challenging part of your job?*

A: I think when a customer is very upset and they're venting and/or making personal attacks. You need to have an understanding that this isn't about me as a person; rather it's about their situation and their frustration. The challenge is to have compassion and empathy while helping them at the same time. By helping them resolve their issues, it helps me grow.

Q: *What are the keys to success to being in customer service?*

A: You need to possess compassion and an appreciation for other people's views. You really need to have an open mind and the ability to put yourself in their place. At the end of the day you need to be able to walk away and find the humor in everything. Even the contentious ones can be a bit silly in their own intensity. People tend to be upset about things that aren't that important in the bigger scheme of things. Having perspective is key.

✔ **Has anybody seen my order?** Customer service representatives typically receive calls regarding the status of orders they've placed. It will be your job to talk to the customer while digging up account information on your computer screen. You may also receive questions regarding a bill statement. Doing at least two things at once is a frequent feature of this job.

What You Can Do Now

✴ Put yourself in an environment that will sharpen your communication and telephone skills. Employers in this field prefer candidates who have experience dealing with the general public.

✴ Pick up some general office skills, such as learning how to transfer phone calls.

✴ Take a typing class. Although your job will center on talking, you will need to take notes about the progress on your accounts— the more comfortable you are with your keyboard, the easier it will be to focus on the other aspects of your job.

✴ If you're interested in either banking or insurance, consult with your local community or business to college to see if they offer coursework relevant to your field of interest.

What Training You'll Need

Training depends greatly on the industry you choose. For example, positions in the insurance industry require a very specific education. If working for a major electronics store, you may have to learn about the stereos, cameras, DVD players, TVs, and iPods that are for sale. For most customer service positions, you can get training on the job and you can begin with a high school diploma, an appetite for talking, and enough computer smarts to dig up information from databases and off the Internet. Most on-the-job training includes an overview of a company's products, procedures, and regulations. New hires may also receive a tutorial on the phone skills and computer systems. As you continue in the career, you will need to keep up-to-date with any regulations and developments that affect your profession.

How to Talk Like a Pro

Here are a few words you'll hear as a customer service representative:

✦ **Customer experience management** This is a term used to describe the methods used to design and manage a customer's total experience with a product, service, or company.

✦ **Competitive advantage** An organization may try to differentiate itself from its competition by providing better customer service. If a company can build a solid reputation for customer care that attracts or retains more customers, your company is establishing a competitive advantage.

✦ **Back order** This is a term referring to the status of an item that is out of stock but on its way to being acquired. For example: "We're out of iPods at the moment. They're on back order."

How to Find a Job

All industries hire customer service professionals, so you may want to start your job search by looking at businesses that interest you. You may love music or cars or outdoor sports. Whatever your interest, there are businesses out there to match, and they all need good customer support. If you can't land a position in customer care right away, you might accept another position to get a foot in the door. Prove yourself at a job stocking shelves or ringing up sales as a cashier and you may be first in line for when a position in customer service opens. Comb the local classifieds and major Internet job sites for opportunities. When applying for positions, present yourself as a good communicator and a good listener. Voice your willingness to work evenings, weekends, and holidays, or some combination thereof. This career has a high turnover rate, so if your first visit to an electronics superstore, cell phone outlet, or department store doesn't result in an interview, try again.

Secrets for Success

See the following suggestions and turn to the appendix for advice on résumés and interviews.

✦ Distinguish yourself! Show that little bit of extra effort or hospitality, and coworkers, supervisors, and customers will remember

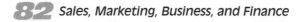

you. That will help your name come up first when it's promotion time.

★ Always listen. Sometimes customers are happy just to have some attention. Treat shopper concerns seriously—you will be surprised how lending an ear can lead to more satisfied customers.

Reality Check

Can you stay calm in the face of anger? Some customers may lose their cool and vent their anger at you. You must have a thick skin and maintain a level head to soothe the dissatisfied customer. A placid attitude shows that you are professional and dignified—qualities that businesses admire.

Some Other Jobs to Think About

★ Insurance sales agent. Insurance sales agents interact frequently with the public, educating consumers about different types of insurance. They have to be good listeners to determine what insurance will best meet a customer's needs. Top agents can earn sizable commissions.

★ Computer support specialist. Computer support specialists field phone calls and offering solutions to customers and clients who are having computer problems. Again, they have to listen carefully to the customer's problems in order to provide the proper technical assistance and advice.

How You Can Move Up

★ Become an insurance sales agent. Reps in the insurance industry may learn enough about products and services to advance to the position of sales agent. Sales agents sell the actual policies and earn commissions on every policy sold.

★ Apply for a store manager position. In a retail customer service position, you master how to keep customers happy, and you learn the daily operations of the store where you work. As you gain a thorough knowledge of your organization and its customers, you become an ideal candidate to manage.

Web Sites to Surf

Customer Service Manager.com This site includes news and articles for customer service managers and professionals, offering helpful advice on an array of topics, including how to handle difficult customers.
http://www.customerservicemanager.com

International Customer Service Association. This site offers two kinds of certification programs, a jobs board, and a nationwide list of chapters.
http://www.icsa.com

Maintain inventory

6

Shipping/ Stock Clerk

Learn store operations

Organize products

Shipping/Stock Clerk

Shipping and stock clerks are order-fillers and order-shippers, keeping shelves stocked and customers happy as they provide a vital function in the retail and wholesale industry. As long as retail superstores, grocery stores, warehouses, wholesale centers, and manufacturing centers produce and sell goods, clerks will be needed to stock and restock items. At warehouses, shipping clerks organize products to be easily packaged, loaded, shipped, and counted. In retail stores, stock clerks put items neatly on display so they're easy to view, take off the shelves, and appear attractive to customers. Although this entry-level position requires only a high school diploma and is relatively easy to get into, the job can be a stepping stone to more advanced careers in management and supervision. Jobs are plentiful, with about 2.3 million clerks employed in the United States, according to 2006 data from the U.S. Bureau of Labor Statistics. As the Internet age and online shopping continue to fuel an ever-expanding appetite for retail goods, positions are expected to multiply in the near future. Better still, most of the training you'll need is provided on the job, so you'll be able to pursue this new career right away.

Is This Job for You?

To find out if being a clerk is a good fit for you, read each of the following questions and answer "Yes" or "No."

Yes	No	**1.**	Can you stand on your feet for long periods of time?
Yes	No	**2.**	Do you have an eye for display?
Yes	No	**3.**	Do you have good eyesight?
Yes	No	**4.**	Are you good physical shape?
Yes	No	**5.**	Are you comfortable handling numbers?
Yes	No	**6.**	Can you work under supervision?
Yes	No	**7.**	Can you lift heavy objects regularly?
Yes	No	**8.**	Can you perform repetitive tasks with precision?
Yes	No	**9.**	Do you possess strong organizational skills?
Yes	No	**10.**	Can you take direction well?

If you answered "Yes" to most of these questions, consider a career as a stock or shipping clerk. To find out more about these jobs, read on.

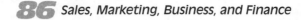

Let's Talk Money

Wages for clerks vary not only by geography but also by specialization. On average, stock clerks earn $9.66 per hour, while shipping clerks earn about two dollars more at $11.73 per hour, according to 2006 data from the Bureau of Labor Statistics. The average annual income of a stock clerk is $20,100, with the top 10 percent earning more than $33,420. On average, shipping clerks make $24,400 per year with the highest 10 percent earning more than $37,600. Most positions in this field offer medical and dental coverage, with two weeks of vacation time.

What You'll Do

As a shipping or stock clerk, your job focuses on the organization, verification, and delivery of merchandise or materials. Your ability to stay on top of the receiving, unpacking, checking, and storage of product is what keeps the cash registers ringing at your local Costco or Wal-Mart. Before you can move up the ladder to warehouse manager, head clerk, or even industrial traffic manager, you need to learn the basics of being a clerk in retail. You must sort, organize, and mark merchandise with identification labels and codes. If you're a stock clerk in a grocery or department store, you spend part of your day transporting cartons of merchandise from the storeroom onto the retail floor. You also devote a considerable amount of time moving materials or merchandise, storing them in bins, on the floor, or on shelves. In addition to the heavy lifting, you do lighter work, using a handheld scanner connected to a computer to log merchandise into the system so as to ensure that an inventory of your product remains current.

While stock clerks spend the bulk of their day moving products from point A to point B, shipping clerks are chiefly record keepers who keep track of incoming and outgoing shipments. Attention to detail and numbers is key. After all, you are the one who verifies that orders have been filled correctly, all the while preparing shipping documents and mailing labels. In addition to being responsible for developing invoices, you must take care of interoffice paperwork as you supply shipment information to accounting or other parts of the company. A word of warning: Computing freight or postal rates is a daily part of this job. So think twice about this field if you are shy around calculators.

Although some of the job is not physically straining—shuffling through records and checking the whereabouts of a shipment on the Internet, the work can require heavy lifting, so you it pays to be physically fit. Some gear—such as forklifts, carts, and dollies—makes the job easier, but still a fair amount of walking, standing, bending, and lifting is required.

Who You'll Work For

* Retail establishments, such as department stores and superstores
* Shipping companies
* Wholesalers
* Grocery stores
* Warehouses
* Factories

Where You'll Work

Your job environment will largely be a function of what type of clerk job you choose. According to the Bureau of Labor Statistics, three out of four clerks work in wholesale and retail settings, including grocery stores, and chains such as Target, PetSmart, and Macy's. Shipping clerks can work in similar work settings, but a great many of these jobs can also be found at wholesale warehouses, shipping depots, or factories. Urban and suburban areas populated by megastores are more likely to offer the most opportunities.

Let's Talk Trends

This is a nation of shoppers, and the surge of catalog, direct mail, telephone, and Internet shopping services has spurred the demand for stock clerks. Opportunities are expected to grow over the next decade, according to the Bureau of Labor Statistics. Openings are continuously becoming available for this entry-level position as clerks move up the ladder into management and supervisory roles.

Shipping clerks generally clock in for day shifts, Monday through Friday, although particularly large shipments can require occasional weekend hours. Evening and weekend hours are more common for stock clerks who have to handle the arrival of large shipments or put in overtime at inventory season. Automated devices have lessened the physical demands of the job, but operating mechanical material-handling equipment—such as pallet jacks for moving heavier items— still takes physical stamina. In general, the larger the company you work for, the more likely you will use labor-saving equipment and computers.

Your Typical Day

Here are the highlights of a typical day as a stock or shipping clerk.

✔ **Keep records of all outgoing shipments.** Prepare mailing labels and shipping documents. Double-check to make sure that orders have been filled correctly. As you process orders, you may need to make a visit to the stockroom to fill the order yourself. You may also need to look up and calculate freight and postal weights while recording the cost and weight of every shipment.

✔ **Fill those orders.** Stock clerks spend their day running through a cycle of receiving, unpacking, and replenishing shelves or filling orders for shipment. Note any damaged or spoiled goods.

✔ **Code your products.** Sort, organize, and mark goods with identifying codes. The easier it is for you to locate your product, the easier it will be to ship. You may use a handheld scanner connected to a computer to ensure that your inventory list is up-to-date.

✔ **Lift with your legs, not your back.** Use the best and most comfortable way to get boxes from point A to point B. When possible, you take advantage of labor-saving devices. Often, you climb aboard a forklift, and load and unload palettes full of cargo.

What You Can Do Now

✶ Look for summer or after-school work that will allow you to develop or strengthen your computer skills.

✶ Take classes in computers, math, and accounting in your high school.

✶ Learn how to use basic office and computer equipment, including photocopiers and scanners.

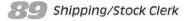

The Inside Scoop: Q & A

Dan Butler
Vice president of merchandising and retail operations
Washington, D.C.

Q: *How did you get your job?*

A: I wanted to get into the operations end of the retail business and this [shipping and stocking] was a good starting point to get in with the company and work my way into a management. I knew that if I worked hard and learned things from the ground up, I would be an asset to the company.

Q: *What do you like best about your job?*

A: Although it's physically demanding, I liked being able to help figure out the best and most efficient way to improve our processes. That way of thinking paid off throughout my career. Sometimes the experience you have on the frontline helps shape the rest of your career path.

Q: *What's the most challenging part of your job?*

A: Keeping up with heavier flow of goods at the holiday season is very demanding. You have to take responsibility for maintaining the efficiency of the operation regardless of the circumstances (someone is out sick, the truck is arriving late, the trash compactor gets backed up, etc.).

Q: *What are the keys to success to being a shipping or stock clerk?*

A: You have to be detail-oriented to make sure every item is processed appropriately every time. You are your own "quality control expert."

✯ Get physically fit. You might even take a part-time job that involves a lot of physical labor and lifting to see if that type of work is for you.

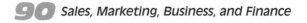

What Training You'll Need

A high school diploma is all you'll need for most shipping, receiving, and stock clerk positions. Jobs solely focused on stocking shelves, freezers, or racks are readily available. However, your chances for getting hired improve considerably if you can demonstrate a familiarity with computers and additional electronic office equipment. For stock clerks in particular, record keeping, typing, filing, and other clerical skills are likely to increase employability. In most cases, your employer provides training and any required uniform. During supervised training, clerks master the ins and outs of counting and marking stock (product), followed by an introduction on how to keep records and take inventory.

How to Talk Like a Pro

Here are a few words to know as a shipping or stock clerk:

* **Inventory** This is a detailed report or survey of all goods and/or materials in stock. Many retail stores do an annual inventory, physically checking to see that every item in the company's records is actually in the store. This review is necessary for tax and budgetary reasons.
* **Invoice** A list of goods or services detailed line by line or itemized. Drawn up for each shipment, this document details all costs for goods shipped or services performed.
* **Bill of lading** This is a document, issued by a carrier to a shipper, that acknowledges the receipt of goods for transport and specifies the terms of the shipment's delivery.

How to Find a Job

To find a job as a shipping or stock clerk, start by looking around your neighborhood to see if there are any retail stores or wholesale businesses that appeal to you. File an application with those operations. If you have previous work experience that includes using office or moving equipment, bring along a résumé of your work history. Don't forget the power of networking. If you know a friend or relative working in retail or production, ask him or her if they know of any openings for clerks. Also, try a search engine or job site such as Monster.com or CareerBuilder.com.

Secrets *for Success*

See the following suggestions and turn to the appendix for advice on résumés and interviews.

✴ Stay organized. It will be your job to retrieve and allocate orders from a computer system, while processing and updating shipping documents. If you can keep track of what you've processed and you know where to find it at a moment's notice, your day will go smoothly. If not, you'd best invest in a bottle of aspirin.

✴ Stay fit. Repeated lifting requires a strong back, arms, and legs. Working out at the gym and maintaining muscle tone will help.

Reality *Check*

Do you have physical endurance and can you handle repetitive tasks? The best clerks take pleasure in the physical and organizational aspects of the profession. Seriously ask yourself if you can handle the rigors of this position.

Some *Other Jobs to Think About*

✴ Cargo or freight agent. Cargo and freight agents perform tasks that are similar to shipping clerks, such as calculating shipping fees and tracking cargo and shipments. This sector focuses on heavy details rather than heavy lifting. Cargo and freight agents are responsible for making sure the proper customs paperwork is in order as they frequently work with shipments via train, plane, and truck.

✴ Procurement clerk. Procurement clerks prepare purchase orders, working also as buyers or purchasing agents at small-to-midsize companies.

How *You Can Move Up*

✴ Become an industrial traffic manager. Those who get their foot in the door at a factory or warehouse and demonstrate a vast understanding of shipping and receiving may find themselves arranging transport for boxes instead of lifting them.

✴ Advance to a head clerk position. Once they've developed a thorough understanding of operations, clerks can be promoted to the supervisory position of head clerk.

✴ Apply for a warehouse manager job. Warehouse managers are responsible for planning and coordinating warehouse operations at the Home Depots, distribution hubs, and manufacturing plants of the world. Talking to clients, planning deliveries, monitoring storage space, and tracking goods are part of this all-encompassing job.

Web Sites to Surf

The National Retail Federation. This site offers an overview of the retail industry, detailing current issues and upcoming conferences on careers. Check out the nationwide listing of skills centers that can help prepare you for a career as a clerk or some other part of product management. http://www.nrf.com

National Association of Wholesaler-Distributors. This site includes frequently asked questions about the wholesale field, providing information about the business of getting products to the market in very large numbers. http://www.naw.org

Unlock your network

Appendix A

Get your résumé ready

Ace your interview

Putting Your Best Foot Forward

When 20-year-old Justin Schulman started job-hunting for a position as a fitness trainer—the first step toward managing a fitness facility—he didn't mess around. "I immediately opened the Yellow Pages and started calling every number listed under health and fitness, inquiring about available positions," he recalls. Schulman's energy and enterprise paid off: He wound up with interviews that led to several offers of part-time work.

Schulman's experience highlights an essential lesson for job seekers: There are plenty of opportunities out there, but jobs won't come to you—especially the career-oriented, well-paying ones that that you'll want to stick with over time. You've got to seek them out.

Uncover Your Interests

Whether you're in high school or bringing home a full-time paycheck, the first step toward landing your ideal job is assessing your interests. You need to figure out what makes you tick. After all, there is a far greater chance that you'll enjoy and succeed in a career that taps into your passions, inclinations, and natural abilities. That's what happened with career-changer Scott Rolfe. He was already 26 when he realized he no longer wanted to work in the food industry. "I'm an avid outdoorsman," Rolfe says, "and I have an appreciation for natural resources that many people take for granted." Rolfe turned his passions into his ideal job as a forestry technician.

If you have a general idea of what your interests are, you're far ahead of the game. You may know that you're cut out for a health care career, for instance, or one in business. You can use a specific volume of Great Careers with a High School Diploma to discover what position to target. If you are unsure of your direction, check out the whole range of volumes to see the scope of jobs available.

You can also use interest inventories and skills-assessment programs to further pinpoint your ideal career. Your school or public librarian or guidance counselor should be able to help you locate such assessments. Web sites, such as America's Career InfoNet (http://www.acinet.org) and Jobweb.com, also offer interest inventories. You'll find suggestions for Web sites related to specific careers at the end of each chapter in any Great Careers with a High School Diploma volume.

Unlock Your Network

The next stop toward landing the perfect job is networking. The word may make you cringe, but networking is simply introducing yourself and exchanging job-related and other information that may prove helpful to one or both of you. That's what Susan Tinker-Muller did. Quite a few years ago, she struck up a conversation with a fellow passenger on her commuter train. Little did she know that the natural interest she expressed in the woman's accounts payable department would lead to news about a job opening there. Tinker-Muller's networking landed her an entry-level position in accounts payable with MTV Networks. She is now the accounts payable administrator.

Tinker-Muller's experience illustrates why networking is so important. Fully 80 percent of openings are *never* advertised, and more than half of all employees land their jobs through networking, according to the U.S. Bureau of Labor Statistics. That's 8 out of 10 jobs that you'll miss if you don't get out there and talk with people. And don't think you can bypass face-to-face conversations by posting your résumé on job sites like Craigslist, Monster.com, and Hotjobs.com and then waiting for employers to contact you. That's so mid-1990s! Back then, tens of thousands, if not millions, of job seekers diligently posted their résumés on scores of sites. Then they sat back and waited . . . and waited . . . and waited. You get the idea. Big job sites have their place, of course, but relying solely on an Internet job search is about as effective throwing your résumé into a black hole.

Begin your networking efforts by making a list of people to talk to: teachers, classmates (and their parents), anyone you've worked with, neighbors, members of your church, synogogue, temple, or mosque, and anyone you've interned or volunteered with. You can also expand your networking opportunities through the student sections of industry associations; attending or volunteering at industry events, association conferences, career fairs; and through job-shadowing. Keep in mind that only rarely will any of the people on your list be in a position to offer you a job. But whether they know it or not, they probably know someone who knows someone who is. That's why your networking goal is not to ask for a job but the name of someone to talk with. Even when you network with an employer, it's wise to say something like, "You may not have any positions available, but would you know someone I could talk with to find out more about what it's like to work in this field?"

Also, keep in mind that networking is a two-way street. For instance, you may be talking with someone who has a job opening that isn't appropriate for you. If you can refer someone else to the employer, either person may well be disposed to help you someday in the future.

Dial-Up Help

Call your contacts directly, rather than e-mail them. (E-mails are too easy for busy people to ignore, even if they don't mean to.) Explain that you're a recent graduate; that Mr. Jones referred you; and that you're wondering if you could stop by for 10 or 15 minutes at your contact's convenience to find out a little more about how the industry works. If you leave this message as a voicemail, note that you'll call back in a few days to follow up. If you reach your contact directly, expect that they'll say they're too busy at the moment to see you. Ask, "Would you mind if I check back in a couple of weeks?" Then jot down a note in your date book or set up a reminder in your computer calendar and call back when it's time. (Repeat this above scenario as needed, until you get a meeting.)

Once you have arranged to talk with someone in person, prep yourself. Scour industry publications for insightful articles; having up-to-date knowledge about industry trends shows your networking contacts that you're dedicated and focused. Then pull together questions about specific employers and suggestions that will set you apart from the job-hunting pack in your field. The more specific your questions (for instance, about one type of certification versus another), the more likely your contact will see you as an "insider," worthy of passing along to a potential employer. At the end of any networking meeting, ask for the name of someone else who might be able to help you further target your search.

Get a Lift

When you meet with a contact in person (as well as when you run into someone fleetingly), you need an "elevator speech." This is a summary of up to two minutes that introduces who you are, as well as your experience and goals. An elevator speech should be short enough to be delivered during an elevator ride with a potential employer from the ground level to a high floor. In it, it's helpful to show that 1) you know the business involved; 2) you know the company; 3) you're qualified (give your work and educational information); and 4) you're goal-oriented, dependable, and hardworking. You'll be surprised how much information you can include in two minutes. Practice this speech in front of a mirror until you have the key points down very well. It should sound natural though, and you should come across as friendly, confident, and assertive. Remember, good eye contact needs to be part of your presentation as well as your everyday approach when meeting prospective employers or leads.

Get Your Résumé Ready

In addition to your elevator speech, another essential job-hunting tool is your résumé. Basically, a résumé is a little snapshot of you in words, reduced to one 8½ x 11-inch sheet of paper (or, at most, two sheets). You need a résumé whether you're in high school, college, or the workforce, and whether you've never held a job or have had many.

At the top of your résumé should be your heading. This is your name, address, phone numbers, and your e-mail address, which can be a sticking point. E-mail addresses such as sillygirl@yahoo.com or drinkingbuddy@hotmail.com won't score you any points. In fact they're a turn-off. So if you dreamed up your address after a night on the town, maybe it's time to upgrade. (And while we're on the subject, these days, potential employers often check Myspace pages, personal blogs, and Web sites. What's posted there has been known to cost candidates job offers.)

The first section of your résumé is a concise Job Objective: "Entry-level agribusiness sales representative seeking a position with a leading dairy cooperative." These days, with word-processing software, it's easy and smart to adapt your job objective to the position for which you're applying. An alternative way to start a résumé, which some recruiters prefer, is to rework the Job Objective into a Professional Summary. A Professional Summary doesn't mention the position you're seeking, but instead focuses on your job strengths: e.g., "Entry-level agribusiness sales rep; strengths include background in feed, fertilizer, and related markets and ability to contribute as a member of a sales team." Which is better? It's your call.

The body of a résumé typically starts with your Job Experience. This is a chronological list of the positions you've held (particularly the ones that will help you land the job you want). Remember: Never, never fudge anything. It is okay, however, to include volunteer positions and internships on the chronological list, as long as they're noted for what they are.

Next comes your Education section. Note: It's acceptable to flip the order of your Education and Job Experience sections if you're still in high school or don't have significant work experience. Summarize any courses you've taken in the job area you're targeting, any certifications you've achieved, relevant computer knowledge, special seminars, or other school-related experience that will distinguish you. Include your grade average if it's more than 3.0. Don't worry if you haven't finished your degree. Simply write that you're currently enrolled in your program (if you are).

In addition to these elements, other sections may include professional organizations you belong to and any work-related achievements, awards, or recognition you've received. Also, you can have a section for your interests, such as playing piano or soccer (and include any notable achievements regarding your interests, for instance, placed third in Midwest Regional Piano Competition). You should also note other special abilities, such as "Fluent in French," or "Designed own Web site." These sorts of activities will reflect well on you whether or not they are job-related.

You can either include your references or simply note, "References Upon Request." Be sure to ask your references permission to use their name, and alert them to the fact that they may be contacted, before you include them on your résumé. For more information on résumé writing, check out Web sites such as http://www.resume.monster.com.

Craft Your Cover Letter

When you apply for a job either online or by mail, it's appropriate to include a cover letter. A cover letter lets you convey extra information about yourself than doesn't fit or isn't always appropriate in your résumé. For instance, in a cover letter, you can and should mention the name of anyone who referred you to the job. You can go into some detail about the reason you're a great match, given the job description. You can also address any questions that might be raised in the potential employer's mind (for instance, a gap in your résumé). Don't, however, ramble on. Your cover letter should stay focused on your goal: to offer a strong, positive impression of yourself and persuade the hiring manager that you're worth an interview. Your cover letter gives you a chance to stand out from the other applicants and sell yourself. In fact, 23 percent of hiring managers say a candidate's ability to relate his or her experience to the job at hand is a top hiring consideration, according to a CareerBuilder.com survey.

You can write a positive, yet concise cover letter in three paragraphs: An introduction containing the specifics of the job you're applying for; a summary of why you're a good fit for the position and what you can do for the company; and a closing with a request for an interview, your contact information, and thanks. Remember to vary the structure and tone of your cover letter. For instance, don't begin every sentence with "I."

Ace Your Interview

Preparation is the key to acing any job interview. This starts with researching the company or organization you're interviewing with. Start with the firm, group, or agency's own Web site. Explore it thoroughly, read about their products and services, their history, and sales and marketing information. Check out their news releases, links that they provide, and read up on, or Google, members of the management team to get an idea of what they may be looking for in their employees.

Sites such as http://www.hoovers.com enable you to research companies across many industries. Trade publications in any industry (such as *Food Industry News*, *Hotel Business*, and *Hospitality Technology*) are also available at online or in hard copy at many college or public libraries. Don't forget to make a phone call to contacts you have in the organization to get a better idea of the company culture.

Preparation goes beyond research, however. It includes practicing answers to common interview questions:

✦ *Tell me about yourself.* Don't talk about your favorite bands or your personal history; give a brief summary of your background and interest in the particular job area.

✦ *Why do you want to work here?* Here's where your research into the company comes into play; talk about the firm's strengths and products or services.

✴ *Why should we hire you?* Now is your chance to sell yourself as a dependable, trustworthy, effective employee.

✴ *Why did you leave your last job?* Keep your answer short; never bad-mouth a previous employer. You can always say something simple, such as, "It wasn't a good fit, and I was ready for other opportunities."

Rehearse your answers, but don't try to memorize them. Responses that are natural and spontaneous come across better. Trying to memorize exactly what you want to say is likely to both trip you up and make you sound robotic.

As for the actual interview, to break the ice, offer a few pleasant remarks about the day, a photo in the interviewer's office, or something else similar. Then, once the interview gets going, listen closely and answer the questions you're asked, versus making any other point that you want to convey. If you're unsure whether your answer was adequate, simply ask, "Did that answer the question?" Show respect, good energy, and enthusiasm, and be upbeat. Employers are looking for workers who are enjoyable to be around, as well as good workers. Show that you have a positive attitude and can get along well with others by not bragging during the interview, overstating your experience, or giving the appearance of being too self-absorbed. Avoid one-word answers, but at the same time don't blather. If you're faced with a silence after giving your response, pause for a few seconds, and then ask, "Is there anything else you'd like me to add?" Never look at your watch and turn your cell phone off before an interview.

Near the interview's end, the interviewer is likely to ask you if you have any questions. Make sure that you have a few prepared, for instance:

✴ *"Tell me about the production process."*

✴ *"What's your biggest short-term challenge?"*

✴ *"How have recent business trends affected the company?"*

✴ *"Is there anything else that I can provide you with to help you make your decision?"*

✴ *"When will you make your hiring decision?"*

During a first interview, never ask questions like, "What's the pay?" "What are the benefits?" or "How much vacation time will I get?"

Find the Right Look

Appropriate dress and grooming is also essential to interviewing success. For business jobs and many other occupations, it's appropriate to come to an interview in a nice (not stuffy) suit. However, different fields have various dress codes. In the music business, for instance, "business casual" reigns for many jobs. This is a slightly modified look, where slacks and a jacket are just fine for a man, and a nice skirt and blouse and jacket or sweater are acceptable for a woman. Dressing overly "cool" will usually backfire.

In general, tend to all the basics from shoes (no sneakers, sandals, or overly high heels) to outfits (no short skirts for women). Women should also avoid attention-getting necklines. Keep jewelry to a minimum. Tattoos and body jewelry are becoming more acceptable, but if you can take out piercings (other than a simple stud in your ear), you're better off. Similarly, unusual hairstyles or colors may bias an employer against you, rightly or wrongly. Make sure your hair is neat and acceptable (consider getting a haircut). Also go light on the makeup, self-tanning products, body scents, and other grooming agents. Don't wear a baseball cap or any other type of hat, and by all means, take off your sunglasses!

Beyond your physical appearance, you already know to be well bathed to minimize odor (leave your home early if you tend to sweat, so you can cool off in private), use a breath mint (especially if you smoke) make good eye contact, smile, speak clearly using proper English (or Spanish), use good posture (don't slouch), offer a firm handshake, and arrive within five minutes of your interview. (If you're unsure of where you're going, Mapquest or Google Map it and consider making a dry run to the site so you won't be late.) First impressions can make or break your interview.

Remember to Follow Up

After your interview, send a thank-you note. This thoughtful gesture will separate you from most of the other candidates. It demonstrates your ability to follow through, and it catches your prospective employer's attention one more time. In a 2005 Careerbuilder.com survey, nearly 15 percent of 650 hiring managers said they wouldn't hire someone who failed to send a thank-you letter after the interview. Thirty-two percent say they would still consider the candidate, but would think less of him or her.

So do you hand write or e-mail the thank you letter? The fact is that format preferences vary. One in four hiring managers prefer to receive a thank-you note in e-mail form only; 19 percent want the e-mail, followed up with a hard copy; 21 percent want a typed hard-copy only, and 23 percent prefer just a handwritten note. (Try to check with an assistant on the format your potential employer prefers). Otherwise, sending an e-mail and a handwritten copy is a safe way to proceed.

Winning an Offer

There are no sweeter words to a job hunter than, "We'd like to hire you." So naturally, when you hear them, you may be tempted to jump at the offer. *Don't.* Once an employer wants you, he or she will usually give you some time to make your decision and get any questions you may have answered. Now is the time to get specific about salary, benefits, and negotiate some of these points. If you haven't already done so, check out salary ranges for your position and area of the country on sites such as Payscale.com, Salary.com, and Salaryexpert.com (basic info is free; specific requests are not). Also find out what sort of benefits similar jobs offer. Then don't be afraid to negotiate in a diplomatic way. Asking for better terms is reasonable and expected. You may worry that asking the employer to bump up his or her offer may jeopardize your job, but handled intelligently, negotiating for yourself may in fact be a way to impress your future employer and get a better deal for yourself.

After you've done all the hard work that successful job-hunting requires, you may be tempted to put your initiative into autodrive. However, the efforts you made to land your job—from clear communication to enthusiasm—are necessary now to pave your way to continued success. As Danielle Little, a human-resources assistant, says, "You must be enthusiastic and take the initiative. There is an urgency to prove yourself and show that you are capable of performing any and all related tasks. If your manager notices that you have potential, you will be given additional responsibilities, which will help advance your career." So do your best work on the job, and build your credibility. Your payoff will be career advancement and increased earnings.